CREATIVE PROBLEM-SOLVING

Creative
Problem-Solving

THE DOOR TO PROGRESS AND CHANGE

Thomas W. Dombroski

toExcel

San Jose New York Lincoln Shanghai

Creative Problem-Solving
The Door to Individual Success and Change

This edition published by toExcel Press,
an imprint of iUniverse.com, Inc.

For information address:
iUniverse.com, Inc.
620 North 48th Street
Suite 201
Lincoln, NE 68504-3467
www.iuniverse.com

ISBN: 1-58348-723-9

*To my wife and daughters and sons,
who encouraged me*

Contents

5

Preface

This book deals with the creative-problem-solving process, an organized approach to problem-solving, which can be applied to human relations, personal problems, scientific problems, social problems, and economic problems.

The creative problem-solving process is composed of five steps, which are: information-gathering and problem definition, coming up with ideas, evaluation of the ideas against a critique, the decision-making process and, most important of all, the implementation of the decision.

The book is written to guide the layman in his search for a method to solve his problems and also serves as a text for the highly educated. What is offered here may be added to, but it will never go out of style.

Problems, problems, problems—every waking day, we encounter problems. The problems confronting us depend on our position in life and our own day-to-day experiences. The concepts offered in this creative problem-solving book are oriented toward the solution of personal problems. Everyone, regardless of his position in life or his background, could use some help in problem-solving. Procedures that I present and review in this book are aimed at making it easier for you to solve your problems. The name of the process is Creative Problem-Solving. It involves the application of the imagination to solving problems. Since we are aiming at a varied audience, I have kept the book at such a level that anyone with any formal education can understand, appreciate, and apply the principles that are offered here. Creative problem-solving is an organized approach to problem-solving that may be applied to human relations, personal problems, scientific problems, social problems, and economic prob lems. All of us search throughout all of our lives for a better method of solving our problems. What is offered here is an organized method for problem solving.

The objectives of this book are to increase your imaginative ability, to aid in developing your problem-solving ability, to increase your idea fluency, to increase your own potential for creativity, and to show you a pattern for successful living.

The easiest way to understand another person and appreciate his problems is to put yourself in the other person's place. This is called *empathy*. Remember this word, as I will be referring to empathy throughout the book. We have four mental capacities: the absorptive, or the ability to observe and apply attention; the retentive, or the ability to memorize and recall; reasoning, or the ability to analyze and judge; and, last, creativity, or the ability to visualize and foresee and generate ideas. Electronic brains can perform the first three functions but not the last function.

In this book, we will attempt to answer the following questions, which I will pose but not answer now. Throughout the book, you will, I am sure, learn the answers to these questions. The questions are:

1. How far is out?
2. Is 1 + 1 always equal to 2?
3. Is there anything that is impossible?
4. Can man create something from nothing?
5. What is truth?
6. What is beauty?
7. How far is down?
8. Where is up?
9. Can we determine our own futures?

As you learn the procedures of problem-solving, I am sure you will see the answers to these questions in your own mind.

Since this book involves the use of the imagination, you who are reading will have to learn through techniques offered here how to use your imagination in a controlled manner to your greatest benefit.

The techniques offered here will allow you to understand and appreciate the creative problem-solving techniques. While all of what I have said may sound unbelievable to you—the reader—I am sure, if you follow through and read the succeeding chapters while I review and counterreview what I have just said, then creative problem-solving will become clear to you, and I know it will be a distinct advantage to you in your daily living.

Why, in this modern and somewhat complicated world of ours, does one family forge ahead faster than another? Why does one man rise faster in the financial area than others? Why is one woman able to live out her years in comfort and security, while another, equally well fixed at one time, must work as long as she is able?

The late financier and statesman Bernard M. Baruch strikes close to the real answer in his "Baruch: My Own Story." Baruch says: "Many men talk intelligently, even brilliantly, about something, only to prove helpless when it comes time to acting on what they believe."

Mr. Baruch is speaking of one of the weaknesses of a democratic society. This inability to act when a sound decision has been reached very often spells the difference between success and failure for people. I will have more to say about decision-making and implementation in succeeding chapters.

What I will be trying to teach in creative problem-solving in the chapters ahead is not necessarily how to achieve financial success, but I am going to try and teach you a pattern for successful living and some practical steps of how to solve your day-to-day problems.

Introduction

Creative problem-solving is the application of the mind in an orderly manner to solving problems. The orderly application of the imagination in solving problems is a relatively new concept in that it is only approximately thirty years since directed effort using the imagination to solve problems has come into limited use.

Potentially, through imagination, we can do almost anything. We can travel the far reaches of space or explore the deepest waters. We can imagine ourselves into or out of most any situation. While it is a powerful tool, it can also be a dangerous tool if uncontrolled.

Creativity as a science applied to problem-solving is new, and credit for much of the work to date must go to people such as Lawrence Miles, of General Electric, and Alex Osborn, of the University of Buffalo.

At the present time, creative-thinking courses are being taught at the University of Buffalo; the U.S. Army Infantry School, Fort Benning, Georgia; General Electric; and Sylvania Electric Products, Inc. Obviously there are other courses that are being taught in other places, some using other names, but all basically trying to achieve the same purpose, that is, to teach a person the proper approach to solving problems.

Creative problem-solving as it is treated in this book can be applied to any type of problem, whether it deals with the highest type of scientific endeavor or the conduct of daily life. Problems are a part of living. Formal education processes, even to the highest degrees, do not, to my knowledge, lay down for guidance a set of principles or procedures for solving problems such as set forth in this book.

13

In the chapters to follow, I demonstrate unique methods, some of which have never been organized together in one package to solve problems. I also review the various methods that can be used to solve problems creatively.

Creative problem-solving is an organized process of reaching solutions to problems by using the imagination to come up with ideas. Ideas alone cannot solve problems. We must bring the intellect to bear on the ideas. Implementation of the ideas is the most important phase of problem-solving. Choice plays an important part in decision-making. Creative problem-solving can be used by individuals or groups, and the person skilled in this technique will use the minds and ideas of others to his advantage.

Quantity does not mean quality, but quantity can breed quality in that, the more ideas you have to choose from, the better chance you have of coming up with good ideas and decisions to solve the problems at hand.

To be creative . . . the solution to the problem or the idea must be new to you. This does not mean that the idea itself must necessarily be new or novel. Many times we have seen ideas come to fruition only to find they are already in existence or have been tried before.

Anyone can be creative . . . if he puts his imagination to work. In the youngest child or the oldest person we can see the workings of creativity.

The intent of this book is to improve the ability one has to solve problems by taking a reasonable, imaginative approach. Techniques will be discussed to accomplish this goal. The extent to which you apply these techniques will determine your success. The old adage "practice makes perfect" also applies to problem-solving.

Creative problem-solving thrives in an uninhibited atmosphere. Avoid negativity in your approach, and try to overcome it in others. It is always easier to shoot down an idea than it is to put it in practice. I cannot stress the importance of avoiding a negative approach.

Roadblocks to creativity come about through a lack of knowledge, habit, or attitudes. The easy way is to say *no*, but the creative way is to say *maybe*.

In the succeeding chapters, I will attempt to show you ways by which you can:

1. Increase your imaginative ability
2. Increase your idea fluency
3. Increase your ability to solve problems
4. Increase your own ability to reach your potential
5. Show a pattern for successful living

I

Principles of Creative Problem-Solving

CREATIVE PROBLEM-SOLVING

The approach to problems in the past and even today is most of the time dictated by expediency. People in the lower echelons of companies are not necessarily paid to solve problems. They are generally paid to do a job. The job requires a certain amount of production per day in order to justify the employment of the individual. It follows, then, that the prime consideration of an employee is to do his job as defined. In recent years, some companies have taken to use of suggestion systems to obtain ideas to improve jobs or processes or products. In this way, a person can creatively contribute more than his job demands. We can, by this type of method, encourage use of their creative ability. All men have creative ability, and the only thing that separates one man from another is his native creative ability. Evidence has been garnered to show that a man can improve his creative ability, but whether he can increase it beyond what he was endowed with is questionable.

Formal education feeds facts to the mind in much the same way we feed facts to a computer. But the computer cannot be creative; it cannot come up with ideas.

Man can be creative; he can come up with ideas if he puts his mind to it, and his degree of fluency in production of ideas is determined by his training in the process of coming up with

17

ideas. In order to solve problems creatively, you must first come up with ideas. This process is called creative problem-solving.

CREATIVE PROBLEM-SOLVING CONCEPTS

Creative problem-solving is as old as man's existence on earth. The record to the present is a record of man's creative accomplishments. Creativity requires facts. The imagination cannot construct when there is no material. Man in his early days on earth had to garner facts, and, as each man found out more about his environment, others could assemble these facts to create new things. "Necessity is the mother of invention" is a phrase we have all heard. Man concentrated on the basics first: food, clothing, and shelter. From there, he tried to improve his lot. Today we have reached the moon, and we are thinking about ways to get to other planets. There is no real end to our searching and reaching out. The mind of man thirsts for knowledge. Our ability to do things will always be limited only by our knowledge of the situation. As man realizes his own inadequacies, he compensates by inventing or creating those things which will overcome his handicaps.

When we look about our surroundings, we picture our problems in the environment in which we exist. If we know of an environment in which we cannot exist and we wish to exist there, we create artificial environment. This can be likened to what is known as a systems-concept approach. Rather than looking at one small part, we analyze the total to determine the problems that need to be overcome in order to achieve success.

CREATIVITY TESTS

There are serious questions as to whether one can measure an individual's creativity potential. We can measure the relationship of one person to another in relation to creativity. We can also measure the improvement to a limited extent in one's creativity upon training. Whether one can improve his total creative potential is seriously questioned.

Psychological writing on creativity is still sparse. Apparently there is much we can learn concerning the creative process. We know that lack of information indicates ignorance of the problem.

There is significantly more written about the common fly than there is about creativity. Yet we will all agree the creative process in man is much more important than the life cycle of the fly.

Creativity testing at this point in time leaves a lot to be desired. Let us hope that more attention is given to this most important subject in the future.

CREATIVE PROBLEM-SOLVING PLAN

Creative problem-solving is a method by which we can analyze any problem and came to a successful conclusion. Many will say that some problems are impossible to solve but this is not true. One of the basics of creative problem-solving is a positive attitude toward solution of the problem at hand.

All problems can be solved, but not all problems are solved to perfection. We can only solve problems to the extent that we have knowledge concerning the problem. The time involved in a solution of a problem is never well defined. It can be short or seemingly unending.

The creative-problem-solving plan involves five phases:

1. Information phase
2. Ideation phase
3. Evaluation phase
4. Decision-making phase
5. Implementation phase

In order to understand the plan, we must analyze its components. Each phase of the plan is important and must be thoroughly understood before one can make effective use of the plan. We will discuss and analyze each phase separately in succeeding chapters.

Information Phase

All five steps of the problem-solving plan are important to the successful conclusion of a problem. We must start by knowing what the problem is and what all the details concerning the problem are. This phase is sometimes called the "information-gathering phase," "intelligence phase," or "background phase." This phase deals with problem identification. We must learn techniques of how to become more sensitive to problems and how to recognize a problem. Many times our failure to recognize a small problem allows it to grow larger until it is all out of proportion to its original size. After we identify the problem, it is necessary to research the problem. We must collect, assemble, and analyze the facts and/or data concerning the problem. Once we have completed this step, we can begin to define the problem. We must analyze the stated problem and break it down into subproblems. Sometimes we find, upon analysis, that the problem is not stated properly or that a subproblem is the real problem. The old adage holds true here, that you can attack only one problem at a time. If, upon analysis, you find there are several problems then you must decide which is the most important and attack the problem separately, using the problem-solving plan. If you are at the problem-definition step and are not sure of the problem definition, you must repeat the identification and research steps. To go ahead without being certain you are attacking the correct problem would be of no value. The statement "spinning wheels but getting nowhere" applies here. In succeeding chapters, we will set down techniques by which all of the above steps can be accomplished.

Ideation Phase

Once you have set down the correct problem and have completed your background work concerning the problem, you can begin the next phase. Ideation involves the use of the imagination. Restriction of the imagination restricts ideas. In this phase you must try to come up with ideas concerning the problem and withhold critique or judgment of the ideas. At this point you are looking for quantity not quality. Techniques include, idea-spurring questions, formulas, combination, making the strange familiar and the familiar strange.

In the ideation phase, all ideas should be listed. Methods of coming up with ideas vary with different people. In the ideation phase, seek out all sources of help to come up with ideas concerning the problem. Such sources may be:

1. People who know something about it
2. Sources of information concerning it
3. Similar problems and how they have been solved
4. Questions you should ask about different aspects
5. All factors bearing on the problem

We shall discuss later many of the known methods of improving idea fluency.

Evaluation Phase

This phase is sometimes called the judgment phase. In this phase we examine the listed ideas and set up a critique that we can weigh the ideas against, for value. In the evaluation phase we screen and classify the ideas, relate and combine compatible ideas, test ideas against meaningful criteria. In succeeding chapters we will elaborate on the evaluation-phase methods.

Decision-Making Phase

In this phase we must take the ideas evaluated to have the greatest score as our decisions. Naturally there will usually be more than one decision. While the highest graded idea usually is the best decision, judgment enters into the final decision. Methods of presenting your decisions will be reviewed later.

Creative-Problem-Solving "How Chart"

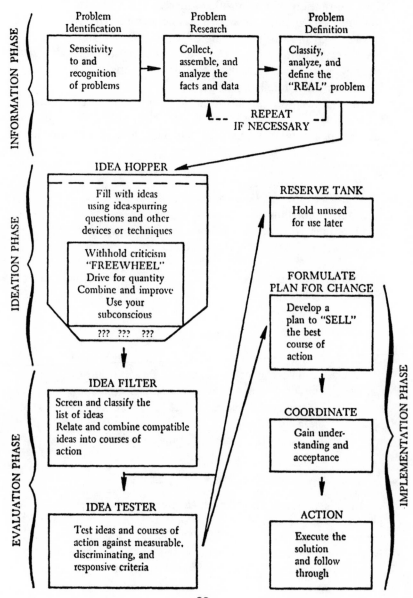

22

Implementation Phase

This phase involves the most important part of the problem-solving plan. All of the prior work can be done and if not implemented the decision has no value. In many cases, projects are stymied at this point because of roadblocks or inaction regarding implementation. In succeeding chapters we will discuss various ways of implementing decisions.

SUPPLEMENT

These problems are presented to teach the principle that you should only apply those restrictions stated in the problem. Do not go by implication or close yourself in with restrictions that do not exist.

Problem of the Pie

How to cut a pie into eight pieces with three cuts:

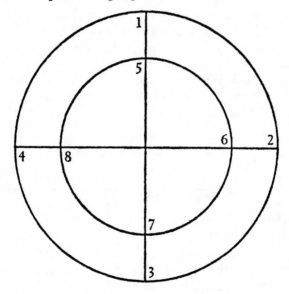

The problem presented is easily solved by making a cross within the pie and then drawing a circle within the pie circle, so that you have eight pieces. Nothing was mentioned about cutting *equal* pieces.

This problem teaches you to think and also teaches you not to put restrictions on the problem that do not exist.

Problem of the Three Fuels

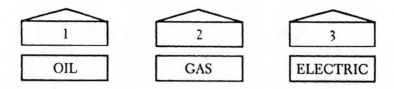

How can we connect each fuel to each house without crossing lines?

The solution is to draw a line from house #3 above and around house #1 and oil over to electric. Then draw a line from house #2 above house #1 and around oil to gas. Then draw a line from house #1 around oil to gas. Then draw lines from oil straight to houses #1, #2 and #3. Then draw a line between houses #1 and #2 and houses #2 and #3. You will now find each fuel connected to each house without crossing lines. No one said the lines must all be straight.

Problem of Getting Ten Horses in Nine Stalls

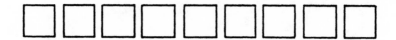

How can we get ten horses in the nine stalls?

For this solution you will find that if you write the words ten horses they will fit in the nine blocks.

Processionary Caterpillars

Processionary caterpillars feed upon pine needles. They move through the trees in a long procession, one leading and the others following—each with his eyes half-closed and his head snugly fitted against the rear extremity of his predecessor. Jean-Henri Fabre, the great French naturalist, after patiently experimenting with a group of the caterpillars, finally enticed them to the rim of a large flower pot. He succeeded in getting the first one connected up with the last one, thus forming a complete circle, which started moving around in a procession, with neither beginning nor end.

The naturalist expected that after a while they would catch on to the joke, get tired of their useless march, and start off in some new direction. But not so.

Through sheer force of habit, the living, creeping circle kept moving around the rim of the pot—around and around, keeping the same relentless pace for seven days and seven nights—and would doubtless have continued longer had it not been for sheer exhaustion and ultimate starvation.

Incidentally, an ample supply of food was close at hand and plainly visible, but it was outside the range of the circle, so they continued along the beaten path.

They were following instinct—habit, custom, tradition, precedent, past experience, "standard practice"—or whatever you may choose to call it, but they were following it blindly.

They mistook activity for accomplishment.

They meant well—but got no place.

The Path of the Calf

One day through the primeval wood
A calf walked home as good calves should;
But made a trail all bent askew,
A crooked trail as all calves do.
Since then three hundred years have fled,
And I infer the calf is dead.
But still he left behind his trail,
And thereby hangs my moral tale.
The trail was taken up next day
By a lone dog that passed that way;
And then a wise bellwether sheep
Pursued the trail o'er vale and steep,
And drew the flock behind him, too,
As good bellwethers always do.
And from that day o'er hill and glade,
Through those old woods a path was made.

The years passed on in swiftness fleet,
The road became a village street.
And this, before men were aware,
A city's crowded thoroughfare.
And soon the central street was this
Of a renowned metropolis;
And men two centuries and a half
Trod in the foot steps of that calf.
Each day a hundred thousand rout
Followed this calf about
And o'er his crooked journey went
The traffic of a continent.
A hundred thousand men were led
By one calf near three centuries dead.
They followed still his crooked way,
And lost one hundred years a day;
For thus such reverence is lent
To well-established precedent.

From "The Path of the Calf" by Samuel Walter Foss, 1895.

II

The Information Phase

BACKGROUND INFORMATION AND
CREATIVE QUESTIONING

In the information phase, we are trying to define the problem. Before we can begin to seek a solution we must ask, "what is the problem?"

In most instances, a problem presents itself in the form of a question. For example, how can we improve the cost factors in our process? This is an example of a production-type problem. In what ways can we reduce the trend of inflation? This is an economic problem statement. How can we help Jimmy improve his school grades? This is an example of a personal problem. In what ways may we reduce the cost of space flights? This is an example of a technical problem. The "how" or "in what ways" preceding a problem prepares the way for creative attack.

The statement of the problem is most important in setting up the problem for attack by the creative-problem-solving method. Once the problem is stated it is necessary to begin to analyze the problem. One method of analyzing the problem is called the "nine-step process." The first step is: Observation—In this step, all the facts about the problem are assembled. Opinions and personal impressions are eliminated. To observe the problem, we use all of our senses. In this way we gain knowledge about the problem. Some of the ways we have of observing facts are: sight, hearing, taste, smell, and feel. Needless to say, mechanical adaptations of the above faculties can be utilized to gather facts for our

27

senses to analyze. In this way additional impersonal methods can aid our problem-solving process.

The second step in the process is: Definition—In order to understand the problem, we must define the problem properly. We must be sure that all of the words in the problem are clear to us before we can really begin to work on the problem.

The third step in the nine-step process is: Preparation—We must gather pertinent data and begin to organize it. Ways in which we can organize data are as follows: arrange in order of time, arrange in order of sequence, arrange in logical order.

The fourth step is: Analysis of the problem—In this method, the problem is broken into parts and studied. We can do this concretely or imaginatively. There are certain methods of analyzing the parts of a problem. Some of the things we do are:

a. Determine the function of parts
b. Compare the influence of parts one on the other
c. Determine the relation of parts to the whole
d. Break down and simplify the problem
e. Determine the most important parts of the problem

The fifth step is: The synectic process—This process, developed by William J. Gordon, divides a problem into two phases. The first phase is to "make the strange familiar." We analyze and study all elements of the problem until we understand the common elements. To make this even more explicit, the problem should now be "old hat," that is, the problem should be as familiar as an old shoe.

To work on developing a more unique solution, we must now "make the familiar strange." To do this, we exploit some apparent irrelevancy to evoke a new viewpoint. For example, if you were to try and think up uses for a pencil other than as a pencil, start by listing things about the pencil that are not necessary. For example, eraser, metal cap, wood, glue, paint, and so forth. Now, to become creative concerning the things that are not necessary, take one of the attributes and think up possible uses for that attribute. For example, the eraser can be used for a rubber bumper on furniture ends.

The sixth step is: The divide-and-conquer procedure—Our minds, it has been said, can only concentrate on a maximum of seven attributes at one time. Therefore, we should, when looking at a problem, consider no more than seven attributes that tend to be intermingled. If we divide a problem into as many parts as possible, we can concentrate more clearly on each part. It has been said that as the extension increases the comprehension decreases. For example, we can picture clearly one tree but it is quite difficult to picture mentally a thousand trees.

The types of problems and the subparts of those problems de-

The seventh step is: Questioning each part of the problem—termine the types of questions that should be asked. For example, if a doctor is examining a sick patient and he is checking his feet, he might ask, "Is the overweight condition of this man compounding his foot problem?" In a problem with a car that steers unevenly, dividing the problem might determine that part of the problem was due to the tire-inflation pressure. In determining the solution to the problem, questioning of the tire pressure might solve this problem.

The eighth step is: Ascertaining the concrete facts—Einstein's theory of relativity might lead us to believe that we should be leery of stating that anything is a proven fact. Our recent successes with trips to the moon have more dramatically shown people that the universe is not a stable situation. To understand our position we will define facts as "concrete things whose elements and attributes we can determine and measure" and "behavior which we can predict with a degree of certainty" and "scientific propositions which are accepted" and "mathematical propositions which are hypothetical but handy," for example, $c^2=a^2+b^2$. When you have determined a specific problem, you should write an explanation of the situation, using extremely specific, concrete, factual language. If possible, point out the facts that make the situation a problem.

The ninth step is: Ascertaining the influential factors—It has been pointed out previously that even problems as factual as engineering problems are more than 75 percent people problems. Unfortunately, it is rarely ever possible to find a problem from which we can entirely eliminate emotional human beings who insist upon red tape, regulations, customs, and even dynamic apathy. These obstacles may not be concrete facts, but they are influential factors and barriers, which must be recognized if they are to be overcome.

ANALYSIS AND SIMPLIFICATION OF THE PROBLEM

As we mentioned previously, there are nine methods of analyzing the problem at hand, using the so-called nine-step process. We use observation, definition, preparation, analysis, the synectic process, the divide-and-conquer procedure, the questioning of each part, the ascertaining of concrete facts, and the ascertaining of the influential factors.

In trying to analyze and simplify a problem, it is necessary to stop and ask, "what is the real problem?" Sometimes a problem is hidden within the actual first-stated problem. It is important to determine which is the real problem.

To aid in analysis of the problem, first try to broaden the problem statement, and then try to narrow down the problem. Examine the problem to see if subproblems are apparent. Determine the most promising problem statement. This then would be the suitable problem for creative attack and therefore the simplified problem.

REDEFINITION OF THE PROBLEM

In many cases the first problem statement is either incomplete or somewhat erroneous. We as human beings have a tendency to mask the real situation. Therefore it is quite clear that, before a problem is submitted to creative attack, we must redefine the problem to be sure we are attacking the correct problem. Restate the problem in a creative-attack manner, and restate parts of the problem. Upon analysis of the restated problem parts, it is then necessary to pick the problem suited for creative attack.

THE SYSTEMS APPROACH TO PROBLEM-SOLVING

In utilizing the systems approach, we mean looking at the total complex problem. For the problem to be solved, we must solve all the subproblems in the system. An example of the systems approach would be the solving of the problem of creation of a nuclear submarine. The problems inherent in the main problem were enormous. In order to solve the main problem, thousands of subproblems needed to be solved. This approach is known as a systems approach to problem-solving.

GOALS IN PROBLEM-SOLVING

The goal in any problem-solving process is the solution of the problem. Aside from the actual goal of problem solution, other goals can be set. For example, we can set goals of cost, time, effectiveness, and so forth. If we do not set goals or evaluative criteria, the solution to the problem can be meaningless.

It is important therefore, in considering the solving of any problem, that the final goal or goals be always kept in mind.

To solve problems just to solve problems is an exercise in futility.

Success

Most people think of success in terms of financial security. This is because we live in a material world. Success can mean, to some people, security, recognition, or achievement. These are nonmaterial measures of success.

Success means many things to many people, but all recognize success as the realization of one's goal.

America today, as never before, is a land of opportunity. There is no other country where one can rise from poverty to become a leader in business and more. We have our country's founders to thank for having the vision and courage to create the government that you and I can enjoy today. In this sense this is a land of opportunity and a sea of success.

Thomas Edison, the great inventor, was a newsboy; Abraham Lincoln, a grocery clerk, who grew up in a log cabin; Henry Ford, a mechanic; John D. MacArthur, the son of poor Scot parents. Thousands have risen from poor circumstances to riches in our United States. Each year more than two thousand men in our country evolve into millionaires.

No matter what your circumstances, you too, can reach your success, be it financial, spiritual, or a combination of both. To succeed, you must start toward your chosen goal in life.

Setting your goal—If you go on a trip without knowing your destination, you may never get to anywhere. As you move toward success you must set a goal. You must decide what you want to do more than anything else. This is not an easy task. You must think it out and apply the principles of creative problem-solving This is an important step, and you should seriously think about it, then firmly fix your goal in mind.

Some people will tell you that the way to arrive at a selection of your goal is to study your likes. What do you like to do better than anything else? What is the one thing you love to do? When you have decided what you like best, this will help point out your goal. When you have determined your best talent, think of how you can use it. If you like to talk to people, you might make a good salesperson, later a good sales manager, and then a sales vice-president.

Once you have decided upon your prime talent and the goal at which you are aiming, then you are ready to prepare yourself for success.

Preparing Yourself to Attain Your Goal

Once you have decided upon your goal, your next step toward success is to begin to prepare.

You must use your present situation as a springboard to your next situation, and that will be aimed toward your goal.

Begin now to educate yourself for this first job in the success direction. Ask yourself what you will need to know to get that job and excel in it. Then get that education.

Night schools offer opportunities for the person with his eye on a goal. Enroll for the courses that will prepare you to succeed in your selected job. Study hard; learn everything you can. Soak up information like a thirsty blotter.

Read all trade magazines pertaining to your chosen field. Read everything you can get your eyes on.

Cultivate people engaged in the field you plan to succeed in. Make them your friends, listen to what they have to say, and profit from their experiences.

When you are prepared, look around for the job you want. Don't be in a hurry. Select the company with care. Make sure its product, its policies and its executives are of the caliber you want to associate with.

Once you have accepted your first job toward your goal, work hard. Give it all you have, and it will pay you back in the long run.

Prepare yourself for advancement, for future responsibilities, by taking on responsibilities beyond your job. Learn everything there is to know about your job and the job ahead.

The price of success is high, but the end is worth the effort. Concentrate on your goal. Live and act your job.

Getting the Right Job

When you have looked around carefully and selected the right job, make a list of the firms you can serve to advantage. Your next step is to get that job with one of those firms.

Make a list of all the things you have to offer the firm to which you plan to apply. Include your education, job experience, and any related experience you may have had. Then go personally to all previous employers and get letters from them addressed to you, stating any experience that would interest your prospective employer. If possible, get samples of any work you have done, and have your previous employers mention any ideas you might have advanced that were successfully used. Get facts and figures.

When you have collected all of this material, write your

resume. Plan your resume from your prospective employer's point
of view. Determine his needs, and show him how you are prepared to fulfill them.

Do not start off with a list of your jobs, or mention your
education and age. Start with a brief account of your highest
achievement that would interest your new employer. Then give a
few more achievements; support these with letters from your
previous employers. Then state how you can serve in your new
job. Then, on a separate and final page, state your past jobs with
dates, your earnings and your education and your hobbies that
point toward success in your new job.

Your next step is to write a brief letter of application. This
should let your future employer know that you have studied his
business and his needs and can be of assistance to him. Then
ask for an interview and an opportunity to show him your
resume.

SECRETS OF SUCCESSFUL PEOPLE

The art of dealing with people is the foremost secret of successful men. Without this key to success, you can have great ability
and education and still only reach mediocrity. With this key,
you can attain far-better-than-average success with only average
ability. You cannot go far alone, but if you can get people to like
you, they will make you more successful than you could ever
make yourself.

Dealing with people is the biggest problem you'll have to
face in your advancement toward success, regardless of your goal.
John D. Rockefeller once said to Mathew C. Brush, ". . . the
ability to deal with people is as purchasable a commodity as
sugar or coffee, and I will pay more for that ability than for any
other under the sun." Nearly every other captain of industry
has made a similar statement.

How, then, do you win people to your side? Rule One:
Treat everyone you meet as if he were important—everyone, without exception. There you have the all-important law of human
relations. If you obey this law, your road to success will be much
easier. If you disobey it, you cannot succeed. William James

wrote, "The deepest principle in human nature is the craving to be appreciated." If you stop to think about this, you will realize that the most important person in your life is you. So it is with every human being. And everyone likes to feel important.

To make people feel important, give them attention instead of trying to attract it. Notice others and let them know it. When you talk with anyone, talk directly to him. Look directly at him. If you talk to the windows or the desk or let your eyes rove around the room, people will get the idea you are not interested in them. Charm comes not from being clever or trying to out-talk or outdo the other person, but by paying close attention to what he says and being deeply interested in him.

Rule Two: Be friendly. Assume that people like you. They will. Smile. Make the friendly advance; don't wait for the other fellow to take the lead. Magnify the good points of everyone. Overlook each person's few annoying qualities and his major ones. A friendly manner wins attention and cooperation beyond the power of purchase.

Rule Three: Let the other fellow do the talking. If you wanted to make friends with a strange dog, you'd speak carefully to it, feed it meat, and rub its head, because dogs like meat and they like their heads rubbed. The same principle applies with people. If you want to win them, give them what they want. People like to talk about themselves, about their problems, their achievements. Let the other fellow do most of the talking. Ask him questions that will start him talking. Be brief yourself but draw him out. And here is a peculiar thing. If you talk a lot, the other fellow will think you a bore and dislike you. If you say only a few words, come to the point of your stories quickly, almost unexpectedly, then stop and listen while he does most of the talking, he will leave you saying what an interesting talker you are, and he will be your staunch supporter.

Rule Four: You can't win an argument. There is a vast difference between a friendly discussion and an argument. You can't win an argument, for, if you win your point, you lose your friend and often make an enemy. To prove a person wrong is to injure his ego, and that is fatal for you. Avoid an argument as you would a rattlesnake. Benjamin Franklin gave this advice,

"If you argue and contradict, you may achieve a victory sometimes, but you never get your opponent's good will."

Abraham Lincoln said, "No man who is resolved to make the most of himself can spare time for personal contention."

Rule Five: Put yourself in the other fellow's shoes. Here's a rule that will work wonders for you if you pursue it constantly. Your friend or fellow worker or the stranger may be absolutely wrong in what he is saying or doing. But, remember, he doesn't think so. Don't condemn him or "tell on him." Try to understand him instead. Ferret out the reason he has for doing what he does. Once you've done that, you have the key to his actions and his good will. Then, along with Lincoln, Roosevelt, and Ford, you will have the only surefire ammunition for getting ahead. You will have a sympathetic grasp of the other man's view.

Rule Six: Practice finding good in people. This is the way to make people like you instantly. It will get them on your side. Don't wait for big things to happen before you praise anyone.

With the next person you see, look for something you can praise, then praise it quickly and naturally. The leader must be generous in his praise for others. He gets credit by giving credit to others. Find good in others, and they will find good in you. Remember, it takes many people rooting for you to make you successful.

Master Yourself

This is probably the most difficult problem you will have to face, and the most important. It is often the difference between success and failure, for if a person cannot master himself he cannot master his job or lead others to work with him.

Fear is the first emotion you will have to master, fear of your own judgment, fear of failure, fear of calling on a prospect, fear of tomorrow, and so on. You do not need to be told that if you walk into a man's office with fear clutching at your stomach with icy fingers, that you will not put yourself across to advantage. He will sense your fear immediately and dislike you intuitively.

How then do you conquer fear? Some of our foremost business leaders have overcome fear by faith and a strong belief in God, others by sheer willpower. Get out and do the things you are afraid to do, do them over and over again until they become second nature with you, until you have built up a record of successful experience. And do not worry about the results.

Worry is another emotion you must master. Worry has been called, by one great industrialist, "the thief that robs you of energy during the night."

Plan your future and keep preparing yourself for opportunities to come by study and work, but actually live one day at a time. In other words, "don't cross your bridges until you come to them." Look back over your life. Isn't it true that most of the things you have worried over have not materialized? Say to yourself each morning, "Today I will do my best in every job that comes my way. I will treat everyone I meet with consideration. I will have some decisions to make, and I will be right most of the time. I will not worry about tomorrow. That will take care of itself."

Industry is the third quality you must master. You will see your friends go off to the movies, to dance, to cabarets, and the urge will be strong to do likewise. But, if you are to succeed, you must pay the high price of success as all other leaders have done. You must work long hours, study into the night, in order to have a high and sustained determination to achieve in spite of all adverse circumstances.

Self-confidence is the fourth quality you must develop, and it comes only after you have mastered the three first discussed. Many successful men have practiced the following rules to win self-confidence:

1. Learn everything you can about your work, so that you are confident of doing your work in a better-than-average way.
2. Control your thinking so that you think only positive and successful thoughts. This takes constant watching and development, but it gives you a confident, successful air.
3. Act as if it were impossible to fail. If you want others to bet on you, act as if you were betting on yourself.
4. Dress carefully so that you look successful, but do not dress to attract attention.

Make a Friend of Your Bank

Successful people consider the bank as one of their best friends. Open a savings account in a good, substantial, progressive bank. Then deposit at least 10 percent of your earnings every payday. Many industrial giants today saved much more than that, making tremendous sacrifices in order to save so they would have cash in the bank to take advantage of opportunities as they presented themselves.

Jacob Franks said, "Good fortune cannot come unless you are provided with capital to seize opportunity when it appears." And thousands of others have stated the same truth.

When your bank account has grown to a thousand dollars, go to your bank and tell them you wish to invest in small bonds. Ask their advice and abide by it.

You might want to purchase a house or a piece of property. Go to your bank and ask their advice. Borrow the necessary money from them, and pay it back on the due date. This will establish your credit. Good credit with a good bank may result in ready money for you to start in business someday or to make an important investment.

There are many other ways in which a good bank can serve you. Get to know the officers personally. Let them know what you are striving for.

You'll be surprised at how they will advise and help you to succeed. They are vitally interested in building businessmen and businesses, for without these they cannot succeed themselves.

Keep a record of all of your expenditures, large and small, so that at the end of the year you can tell whether or not you are saving as much as you should. Ask your bank's advice on budgeting your expenses.

What Great People Have Said about Success

Charles Schwab frequently said that he was paid the largest part of his million-dollar salary because he knew how to deal with people. "I consider my ability to arouse enthusiasm among men," Schwab said, "the greatest asset I possess, and the way to develop the best in a man is by appreciation and encouragement. I never criticize anyone. If I like anything, I am hearty in my praise."

Mathew C. Brush, a former newsboy who rose to head the American International Corporation, said, "The one thing that has helped me the most is that I have always looked for things to do that my superior had been in the habit of doing. I tried to anticipate his every move, every wish, to keep ahead of him in everything, even to getting to the office ahead of him."

Frank A. Vanderlip, president of the National City Bank of New York, said, "The one quality I seek when employing a twenty-five-thousand-dollar-a-year man is personality. He must know how to deal with people successfully."

Mrs. John Dwight, who took over her husband's small business at his untimely death, raised his family, and built the business to a twenty-million-dollar concern said, "Faith in God and in my fellowmen was what carried me through to success, plus a capacity to work harder than any man who worked with me." Notice that Mrs. Dwight said "worked *with* me." She did not say "*for* me." And that probably was her great secret.

Jim Farley said, "Make it a point to learn people's names, and never miss an opportunity to call them by name. I can call fifty thousand people by their first names."

In conclusion, successful men say this, "Make the other man, every other man, any other man, feel bigger. Other men in return will build you bigger that you could ever build yourself." This has been the pattern of successful people through the past.

SUPPLEMENT

Guides to Good Management

1. Perfect your self-control
2. Appreciate and praise
3. Stress rewards; avoid punishment

4. Criticize tactfully
5. Always listen
6. Explain thoroughly
7. Consider your associate's interest as your own

How We Spend Time

sleeping	23 yrs.	32.9%
working	19 yrs.	27.2%
amusement	9 yrs.	12.8%
religion	1 yr.	1.4%
eating	6 yrs.	8.6%
traveling	6 yrs.	8.6%
being sick	4 yrs.	5.7%
dressing	2 yrs.	2.8%
	70 yrs.	100.0%

Quotable Quote

"The future belongs to those men with vision."

Time

When I was only just a lad,
It seemed that time was all I had.
As I passed through my boyhood days,
Time it seems with me had stayed.
When into my teenage years I had grown,
I really felt that time had flown.
Then a young man I became,
And time there was not enough each day.

In my early manhood years,
Time passed quickly sometimes with tears.
The years of middle age had shown,
That time was something I had known.

The early forties life became,
A sort of kind of waiting game.
The fifties brought me no despair,
For I knew that time was still with me there.

In the sixties I then knew,
That time had swiftly passed me too.
And as old age upon me crept,
Time weighed for me as with all the rest.

Then I found as the end grew near,
That time is precious, real, and dear.
So keep in mind as you go through life,
That time is an integral part of life.

Live out your life,
But not in fear,
For time will surely pass
For all of us here.

What should be done?
Why is it necessary?
How should it be done?
When should it be done?
Who should do it?
What are specific goals?
How can I pinpoint the problem?

*   *   *

Look first at yourself to see if you hold biases which could influence your decision.

Listen—your interest may influence answers and uncloud issues that could prove meaningful.

III

Techniques of
the Information Phase

OVERCOMING ROADBLOCKS TO IMAGINATIVE
AND INTELLIGENT CHANGES

The road to success is never easy. This statement is as true today as it was in the beginning when man first appeared on earth. The problems today, though more sophisticated, are in essence no different from those of early man. Our basic aims are to improve and refine for all people the three basic necessities: food, clothing, and shelter. Refinements of these basics create many problems.

There will always be those who will want the easy way out— "the roadblockers." Their guides are such statements as, "It works now—why change it," "Don't rock the boat; it takes too long; it's too hard; it's been tried before; our costs are in line with budget." The creative individual is never satisfied with roadblock statements or status quo. He wants to know why, how, and in what ways things which are stagnant can be improved.

To overcome roadblocks you must do a selling job. A positive approach to the problem will overcome most roadblocks. Sometimes the most difficult part of solving a problem is overcoming the resistance to attack the problem. The creative techniques you will learn in this book are the tools you can use most effectively to overcome roadblocks to progress and problem-solving.

FUNCTION, COST, AND WORTH—AS THEY RELATE TO VALUE AND PROBLEM-SOLVING

In all types of human endeavor there are functions taking place which show themselves either in product or service. Function consists generally of two parts. The one part enhances its performance and the other part enhances its salability. The value or worth of a product or service is the lowest combination of designs, materials, and processes that will reliably perform the functions. In creative problem-solving, the objective is equivalent performance at lower cost. Cost is related to the function, service, or operation purchased by that cost. Creative problem-solving, applied to production problem-solving, is called value analysis.

Our digression into this area of value analysis is only to show that creative-problem-solving techniques can be utilized in many diverse areas of life.

What Is Value as It Relates to Problem-Solving

Value means a great many things to a great many people, because the term value is used in a variety of ways. Also, it is often confused with cost and with price.

In most cases, value to the producer means something different from value to the user. Furthermore, the same item may have differing value to the same customer, depending upon the time, the place, and the use.

Value, then, is a broad term. It can, however, be divided into various kinds of value. It is often divided into four kinds, which are here listed.

Use value: The properties and qualities which accomplish a use, work or service.

Esteem value: The properties, features, or attractiveness that cause us to want to own it.

Cost value: The sum of labor, material, and various other costs required to produce it.

Exchange value: Its properties or qualities that enable us to exchange it for something else we want.

Value is not inherent but is determined by a number of things. To be useful in identifying and eliminating unnecessary cost, value becomes a measure of the appropriateness of the costs involved. Value is stated as the minimum dollars which must be expended in purchasing or manufacturing a product to create the appropriate use and esteem factors.

Value of a product may be considered the cost to accomplish the use and to provide the proper esteem. We are concerned with use value as the lowest cost of providing for the reliable performance of a function, and with esteem value as the lowest cost of providing the appearance, attractiveness, and features that the customer wants.

Maximum Value: Maximum value is never achieved. The degree of value in any product depends upon the effectiveness with which every usable idea, process, material, and approach to the problem have been identified, studied, and utilized.

Normal Degree of Value: In normal usage, value is considered good, if the product contains somewhat better combinations of ideas, processes, materials, and functions, costwise, than competition; it is considered bad, if, because the opposite is true, lost sales volume results. It is readily seen that this method of determining the degree of value comes too late and has serious limitations.

Selected typical products have been subjected to a concentrated and overnormal amount of attention in order to determine more nearly the amount of unnecessary cost they contain when compared, not with competition, but with the optimum combination of available ideas, processes, materials, and design concepts. Such studies have shown that unnecessary cost which can be so identified varies between 25 and 75 percent of the product cost.

The reader must recognize that these unnecessary costs are not hanging like pears from a pear tree for those who wish to pluck, but, rather, that identification and removal are the reward for a well-organized effort, utilizing effective, value-oriented tools and involving appropriate use of money and competence.

Importance of Value

In a free enterprise system, success in the business world hinges on continually offering the best value for the price asked. Competition determines in what direction one must go in setting the value content in order for a product or a service to be competitive with that offered by others.

The best value is determined by performance and cost. It has been generally recognized that an acceptable product must serve the customer's needs and wishes. That is to say, the product must have performance capability. In recent years, it has become clearer that the cost of producing must be such that the customer can buy the product at a competitive price.

REVIEW OF CASE STUDIES

In a recent news article, a case was related concerning a seminar attended by eighty medical doctors. The seminar concerned the use of hypnosis in medical treatment. As part of the seminar, an experiment was conducted in which the eighty participants were to be placed in a hypnotic trance by the lecturer, a skilled medical hypnotist. Of the eighty participants, only one doctor was able to resist the hypnotist. I relate this story to show the great power some individual minds can have over others. The eighty doctors had an education level of at least eight years of college training; yet these highly trained individuals could not resist the hypnotist and therefore came under his control. The mind of man, it seems, has no limit in controlling other men or creating new things or ideas. What we are studying is the use of the mind and its faculties in solving problems.

Let us examine the influence of three other men's minds on other people. In a comparison of John Kennedy, Hitler, and Napoleon, we might say that here were three diverse individuals. Yet these three men had one thing in common, an ability to control men's minds. While Hitler was oriented toward evil, and John Kennedy toward good, Napoleon seemed to be in the middle, between good and evil. The ability all three men had in common was an ability to control men's minds, i.e., they had an ability to get people to like them to extreme proportions.

I relate this comparison of three people only to show that there are certain people who can again control men's minds. Whether they are bent in their control toward evil or good is another matter. We are only trying here to show that people's minds are, to some degree, a powerful tool in shaping the way of the world over other men.

Jules Verne has said, "Whatever one man is capable of conceiving, other men will be able to achieve." As we well know, many of Jules Verne's predictions have come true.

It has been said that man's body is faulty, and his mind untrustworthy, but his imagination has made him remarkable.

INFORMATION PHASE PROBLEMS

The information phase of creative problem-solving deals with the identification of the problem. Most often, the initial problem statement is not correct. To elaborate, the problem statement is either deficient or contains more than one problem. Before starting to creatively attack the problem, it is necessary then that a correct problem statement is made to prepare it for problem-solving.

Once the problem that is to be solved is selected, then the following steps are taken. All available data and facts bearing on the problem are listed. After all facts are collected, the problem-solver gathers together his thoughts and begins to classify and analyze. The problem is then redefined if necessary. At this point it is necessary that you at least look at the problem in terms of its needs for redefinition.

There are three general types of problems: the judicial, fact-finding, and the creative.

Judicial and fact-finding problems are generally not suited to the creative-problem-solving methods. The information desired is too clear cut and requires little or no imagination.

Examples:

a. Judicial problem—What is the color of the wall?
b. How can I get selected for the Naval Academy?—Fact-finding problem.
c. In what ways can we improve the profitability of the business? —Creative-type problems.

In what ways can we coordinate the efforts of social security and the welfare system?

In what ways can we reduce the overall costs of producing light bulbs?

Collecting the facts and data bearing on the problem and a clear restatement of the problem is necessary before proceeding with the further steps in creative problem-solving.

CREATIVE PROBLEM-SOLVING BY INTUITION

Recently I attended a meeting where the speaker was a newly elected school director. The unusual thing about this was that the school director was a woman. The first woman elected to this particular school board was also unique in that this was her first venture into political office. I must admit that I was quite impressed in regard to her presentation regarding the reasons for her venture into politics. She unknowingly used the creative-problem-solving procedure that we are studying to make her decision and implement her decision. In her talk, she went through the process of researching the problem, she came up with ideas on how to solve the problem, she evaluated her ideas against a critique and she made a decision. She then went into the methods she used to implement her decision.

Interestingly, she had never heard of creative problem-solving or using the imagination to solve problems.

I cite this case and share it with you to show you that creative problem-solving is not a unique or new idea but an organization of existing methods to solve problems in a unique logical manner. This woman was the first person I had met who, without training such as you are experiencing, formalized a procedure for solving her problems. Might I say that, if she uses this procedure on her other problems, she will arrive at the best solutions to her problems; where she will be deficient is in the training you are experiencing, where you will learn many of the methods used for all of the five steps in the problem-solving process.

Answers to problems are not difficult to come by, but logical workable solutions will never be easy to come by. Using the problem-solving plan will make the solutions to your problems easier, and you will, by being skilled in the process, be far above others in your ability to solve not only your own personal problems but also to suggest solutions, when asked, to other people's problems. You will be recognized as a problem-solver—a distinction not too many people in this world share.

Let me now tell you about "My Farewell Car." This car was designed by R. E. Olds, and this is what he had to say approximately forty plus years ago about Reo the Fifth:

MY FAREWELL CAR
By R. E. Olds, Designer

REO THE FIFTH—the car I now bring out—is regarded by me as pretty close to finality. Embodied here are the final results of my 25 years of experience. I do not believe that a car materially better will ever be built. In any event, this car marks my limit. So I've called it My Farewell Car.

In regard to Reo the Fifth, we know that this car was not close to finality, nor is it materially better than present cars being built. We also know, in comparison to cars of today, it is really inferior in design, structure, and safety factors. Reo the Fifth is certainly not the ultimate in cars. I say this about the "Farewell Car" to demonstrate that there is no such thing as perfection here on our earth, and everything we see, say, or do can use refinement. In today's world, there are more opportunities than ever before to be creative. Remember what we said previously, that the raw materials of creativity are knowledge and imagination. With the increase in the number of new things that come into being, so also we increase our ability to come up with new and different combinations of the existing things.

I would like to quote from an article by Charles F. Kettering, *"How Can We Develop Inventors?"* This article was written in 1943, and the ending is as follows:

> If we can just achieve the broad outlook and be honest with ourselves and admit that the things we know are so small compared with the unknown, I think we will see that there is no end to progress. I am not worried about the libraries we have today—I am worried about those infinitely greater libraries that haven't any books in them yet. Every year is going to add new things and new books that we don't know. I am interested in getting some of those books written. We should dateline every bit of information we have. We should say, "This is what we know as of today." We shouldn't worry about what it was yesterday—or what it is going to be tomorrow. We should recognize that ideas change and grow, and we should gear ourselves to the most progressive thinking. If we can do that successfully, we will have no difficulty in teaching men to become inventors, because inventing is simply a *state of open-mindedness.*

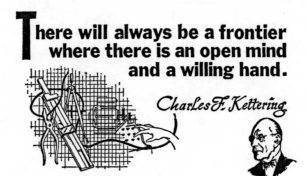

There will always be a frontier where there is an open mind and a willing hand.

Charles F. Kettering

ROADBLOCKS

1. It's been done that way all throu⌐ ne years, why change now?
2. I know it won't work.
3. That's Joe's job, not mine.
4. We can't pay for the tools.
5. Cost isn't important, just get it out the door.
6. We can't help it, it's policy.
7. Not enough time.
8. We don't do it that way in our plant.
9. It just costs too much.
10. That's been tried before.
11. It's too late now, the contract is going to end.
12. Our business is different.
13. We'll come back to it later.
14. It's just not practical.
15. We're making a profit.
16. It leaves me cold.
17. We're over the budget now.
18. Let's think about it some more.
19. Let someone else try it first.
20. We haven't time for details.
21. They won't hold still for that.
22. This isn't the right time for it.
23. We're not ready for it yet.
24. It just doesn't fit in with our plans.
25. We can't hold up production for that.

THE ENGINEER SAYS:
"We'll have to get it from Smith Company
they're the only reliable suppli ers "

THE FACTORY MAN SAYS
"We can't use that finish,
they won't buy it. "

THE ACCOUNTANT SAYS:
"We can't make it that way,
it won't work."

DETOUR

51

SUPPLEMENT

Problems

I would like you to consider the solution to the following problem: If a car is going up a one-mile hill at 30 m.p.h. and gets to the top, how fast does he have to go down the other side, which is one mile, to average 60 m.p.h. over the trip?

Another problem to consider is as follows: A monkey is in a 30-foot well at the bottom, and, when he tries to jump up to get out, each time he jumps up 3 feet, he slides back 2 feet. How many times must he jump in order to get out of the well?

These problems are presented with the idea that they will stimulate your thinking, which is an integral part of problem-solving.

The Lesson of Samuel Clemens

Samuel Clemens or Mark Twain was a fool for any idea that came along that promised instant wealth. The lesson we can learn from his misadventures is to think out clearly any ideas proposed as get-rich-quick schemes.

One of the schemes in which he invested heavily was a type-setting machine. While the idea advanced by the inventor whom Sam subsidized was sound, the complexity of the mechanics was beyond the inventor's capability. Each time the machine was supposed to be ready to demonstrate, something would happen, and a breakdown would occur. The competition heard of this machine and offered to buy out a portion of Mr. Clemens's interest. He would not hear of selling his interest. Finally, after many years of failing to get an operating machine and expending many millions of dollars, Mr. Clemens went bankrupt. He had to work many years to recover from this fiasco.

So, how does this teach us anything about problem-solving? First, Mr. Clemens was depending on someone else to solve his problem, a serious error. Secondly, Our problems, while we can get help, remain our problems. To the extent we can apply sound problem-solving procedures, we will obtain sound results.

Case Studies

After reading the stories of more than a hundred great thinkers spanning the period of 1955 B.C. to the present time, I have found it apparent that all creative people have certain things in common:

1. They are persistent
2. They have unequal driving forces
3. They have clear goals
4. Material success is secondary
5. They are idealistic by nature
6. Most have experienced great trauma or significant life experiences
7. They tend to be introverted
8. They are sensitive people
9. They have great insight
10. They are immediately distinguishable from the masses
11. They are doers
12. They don't give up
13. They don't worry about what other people think of them
14. They are busy people

IV

Developing Creativity

IMPORTANCE OF A POSITIVE ATTITUDE

Creativity requires a positive attitude, and the positive attitude is a characteristic of creative people. There is nothing that is impossible. An attitude of this type aids one in the creative-problem-solving process.

There are certain factors that tend to hinder creativity. Almost any proposed idea can be shown to be wrong, but the problem-solver will look for the ways an idea can be implemented and the problem solved.

The human mind is both judicial and creative. Our judicial mind analyzes, compares, chooses, while the creative mind visualizes, foresees, and generates ideas.

Both methods of thinking require analysis and synthesis. Judgment confines itself to the facts at hand, and imagination reaches out to the unknown.

Judgment will grow with age, whereas creativity will dwindle unless it is kept up by the individual through practice.

Education strengthens judgment, and, the more knowledge we gain, the quicker we are to judge a situation.

Imagination tends to contract as knowledge and judgment expand. Knowledge and judgment cramp creativity unless you are conscious of what is happening.

Judgment looks to the negative whereas creativity calls for a positive attitude.

FLEXIBILITY IN PERFORMANCE

We must be flexible in our performance. There is nothing that is impossible to the creative person.

Imagination is the key to creativity, and we must give it priority over judgment in solving problems. In the five-step process of creative problem-solving we must be flexible and withhold judgment until the fourth step, or decision-making step, is resolved, then apply judgment.

Idea fluency can be developed by not closing the mind to problems. Keeping an open mind during the investigation phase is most important. Do not let habits or well-established concepts deter your idea formation as applied to the problem at hand.

As we mentioned previously, concerning success, people pay highly for two things (1) the ability to lead people, (2) the ability to solve problems.

If you are effective in one or both of these areas, your success in life will be assured. Actually, the second ability is more important than the first, for, remember, we have mentioned previously that problems are a part of daily living, and one of the most important things in life is to be able to solve your daily problems or know where to look for the solution.

IDEA FLUENCY

Ideas are elusive as smoke. If you do not capture them by writing them down, they will disappear. Ideas are the raw material from which great things appear. It follows then that the production of ideas, or idea fluency, is important to what we call progress or change. Things can get better or worse by ideas, but without ideas there is inaction and lack of progress. A good comparison would be the movement of a caterpillar to the movement of a rocket, the caterpillar designating lack of ideas, and the rocket designating progress by the introduction of ideas. Naturally, the wrong ideas can reverse the rocket or the caterpillar.

Ways in which ideas can be encouraged or multiplied are as follows. These are thought starters:

1. What else will do the job?
2. What does that cost?
3. Can we eliminate the part?
4. Can we simplify it?
5. Can we use standard items?
6. Can we use a lower-cost material?
7. Can we use a lower-cost process?
8. Can we use a higher-cost material or process which by its nature or properties will afford a simplified design and facilitate lower-cost assembly?
9. How does it compare to other methods of production?
10. Can it be altered so a high-speed method can be used?
11. Have we generated every possible solution to the problem?
12. Have we consulted all others who may help us?
13. Have we systematically explored advance materials, parts, and processes?
14. Can the part be rearranged?
15. Have we investigated other companies' specialty products and processes?
16. Have we always encouraged free use of our imaginations?
17. Have we recorded every suggestion that seems even remotely possible?

IDEAS AND REALITY

How many times have you heard someone say, "Listen to this great idea"? If you are the average person, you have heard this statement many times from many people. But, how many people realize that there is a great difference between ideas and reality?

Between idea and reality there is a gap. The distance, complexities, character, and definition of the path between idea and reality is never well defined. Most people who voice an idea never realize they are only at the second step in problem-solving when they voice the idea.

The work begins when the idea is voiced and ends with implementation (reality) of the idea.

As Edison said in his pursuit of discovery, "An idea is only an idea until the problem is solved." Too many times, people who voice an idea give up as soon as they discover that an idea is only the beginning of work toward reality.

Ideas are the threads out of which reality is woven, but, as we all know, weaving takes work and skill. It is the skill of the person who works on the idea that finally defines the work needed to reach reality. From Edison's idea of the light bulb to actual creation of light, there was a difficult road to reality. Edison knew that each failure was a step closer to success.

Perseverance on the road from idea to reality will overcome roadblocks and lead you to the success of reality.

INSIGHT

Insight is the ability one has to look into the complexities of a problem and reduce it to a simplified solution. All of us have different insight ability just as we all have different native creative ability.

One's insight into a complex problem or series of problems and his ability to see through the maze are traits that can be developed. As you develop your ability to solve problems using the creative-problem-solving process, your insight into a problem and its apparent solution will amaze your friends. The reason you will be able to perceive the problem and its solution is that, by developing your mind you can cast aside all the extraneous items complicating the problem and get down to the so called nitty-gritty.

You will be able to do this almost automatically as you train yourself in problem-solving, and this develops your insight.

Insight in a person, like creativity, can be either native insight or insight developed by training, refining, and enlarging.

INGENUITY

Ingenuity is another characteristic of a creative person.

Can ingenuity be developed beyond what one has within his own being? This is variable, just as creative potential in a human being is variable. We know that individuals such as Edison, Kettering, Einstein, and others had ingenuity or the ability to devise things they needed to further their work.

Some people you have met through life can be described as possessing ingenuity. Just as we say that creativity may be inborn in a person but not apparent till he is trained to bring it out, so we can say the same about a person who appears ingenious.

One thing we do know is that the person who is skilled in creative problem-solving will exhibit ingenuity. Whether he possessed the characteristics prior to becoming skilled in problem-solving is a moot point, just as whether he has, by improving his creative-problem-solving ability, improved his ingenuity.

INVENTIVENESS

As we examine the lives of inventors, we can only come to the conclusion that inventiveness is important in decision-making and problem-solving.

When we go through the problem-solving process and come to the decision-making phase, simply because we arrive at a decision, should our mind stop and use the decision that first comes to mind? The answer is no; we must raise our inventive ability to go back over our process in arriving at the decision and reexamine with an inventive mind whether we can combine, rearrange, or alternate the problems, the ideas, the evaluation matrices and other elements to determine if the decision we have come to is the best possible one. Time and the circumstances at hand will determine how much more inventiveness we can apply to our problem and decision prior to implementation.

The truly skilled problem-solver stops searching and groping only after the implementation is complete.

Inventiveness can be applied and reapplied as we go back and forth through the problem-solving process.

The true scope of inventiveness presumes a continuous refining of the problem and its solutions even through implementation. There is no such thing as a "finished" problem.

IMPORTANCE OF INNOVATIVE ALTERNATIVES

As an aid to problem-solving it is important to develop alternatives. In order to help you develop alternatives during the problem-solving process, it is important to be able to come up with ideas.

Developing Innovative Alternatives
(Creatively Approaching Your Problems)

1. Study and know yourself: your weaknesses, your strong points, your interests.
2. Broaden your interests: develop a creative hobby, such as music or painting.
3. Talk with strangers and friends. Someone else's ideas may trigger a new one for you.
4. Read and read some more. Improve your reading abilities.
5. Do mental exercises daily: read puzzle books and whodunits.
6. Recognize the value of words, and create word exercises as you read.
7. Ask yourself a new question each day, and try to find the answer.
8. Challenge yourself daily to think up five new improvements that can aid you on the job or at home.

9. Learn to make fantastic and unrelated associations. Be daring and adventuresome, striving for the wild and visionary ideas that are not a part of your workaday world.

10. Use two "idea" notebooks: Carry one on your person and leave the other at the side of your bed.

   a. Write down everything that pops into your mind, no matter how ridiculous it may seem.

   b. Take an idea you have written, and start writing all the variations of it that you can think of.

   c. When you can't think at all, take any subject and start writing about it. This procedure will get your mind circulation working.

   d. Don't throw away rejected ideas. Go over them the next day with a fresh point of view—you might get some good ideas the "second time around."

11. Start a "grab bag" of ideas. Whenever an idea strikes you, write it down and file it away in a large manila envelope. A periodic search through the folder can encourage a chain reaction of more ideas.

12. Establish a definite time each day to think. Pick out a place where your thoughts will be free from interruptions.

13. Brainstorm individually, and in a group, at every available opportunity—it encourages a steady flow of ideas.

14. Reduce as much of your idea search to what you might call routine. Use checklists adapted to your particular kinds of problems.

15. Don't restrict your thinking to your job—use your creative power at home, at play, and with your children.

16. Fix a deadline, and try to meet it.

17. Practice—constantly, diligently. Every creative faculty thrives on use. Turning out ideas is habit-forming.

As a spur to aid in the choice of alternatives, various creative aids and alternative-developing aids are presented here.

CREATIVE THOUGHT STARTER

PUT TO OTHER USES: New Ways To Use As Is?

MODIFY: Change Sound?

MINIFY: Split Up?

COMBINE: How About An Assortment?

SUBSTITUTE: Other Approach?

MAGNIFY: Multiply?

SUBSTITUTE: Other Ingredient?

COMBINE: How About A Blend?

RE-ARRANGE: Other Sequence?

REVERSE: Turn Other Cheek?

ADAPT: Does Past Offer Parallel?

MODIFY: Change Shape?

COMBINE: Combine Ideas?

MAGNIFY: Exaggerate?

ADAPT: What Other Idea Does This Suggest?

SUBSTITUTE: Who Else Instead?

WHY DOES
IT HAVE
THIS SHAPE?

WHAT IF THIS
WERE LARGER?
HIGHER? WIDER?
THICKER?
LOWER?
LONGER?

HOW CAN THIS
BE MADE
MORE
COMPACT?

WHAT IF IT
WERE MADE
LIGHTER
OR
FASTER?

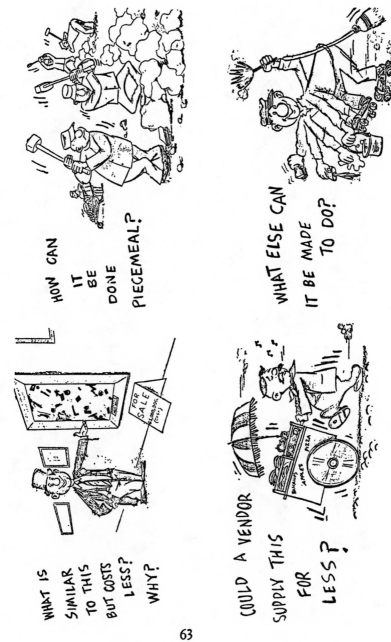

HOW CAN
IT
BE
DONE
PIECEMEAL?

WHAT ELSE CAN
IT BE MADE
TO DO?

WHAT IS
SIMILAR
TO THIS
BUT COSTS
LESS?
WHY?

COULD A VENDOR
SUPPLY THIS
FOR
LESS?

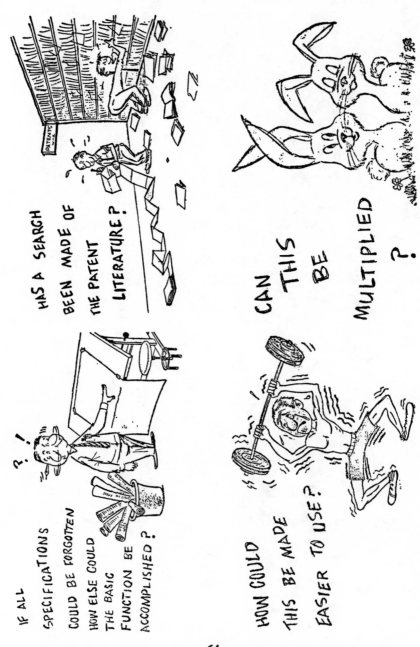

HAS A SEARCH
BEEN MADE OF
THE PATENT
LITERATURE?

IF ALL
SPECIFICATIONS
COULD BE FORGOTTEN
HOW ELSE COULD
THE BASIC
FUNCTION BE
ACCOMPLISHED?

CAN
THIS
BE
MULTIPLIED
?

HOW COULD
THIS BE MADE
EASIER TO USE?

64

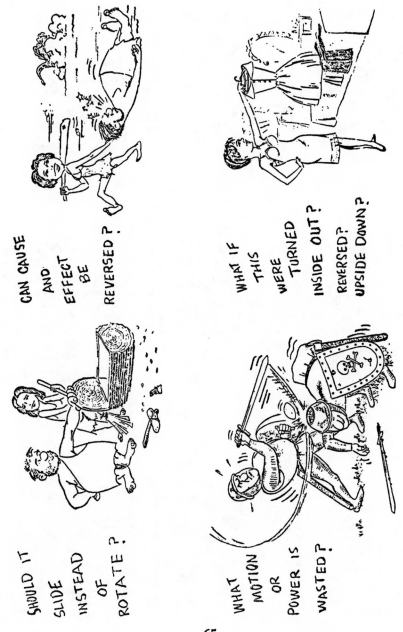

CAN CAUSE
AND
EFFECT
BE
REVERSED ?

WHAT IF
THIS
WERE
TURNED
INSIDE OUT ?
REVERSED ?
UPSIDE DOWN ?

SHOULD IT
SLIDE
INSTEAD
OF
ROTATE ?

WHAT
MOTION
OR
POWER IS
WASTED ?

65

Does its use contribute Value?

Is its cost proportionate to its usefulness?

Is anyone buying it for less?

Does it need all of its features?

Can a usable part be made by a lower cost method?

Will another dependable supplier provide it for less?

Is there anything better for the intended use?

Is it made on proper tooling— considering quantities used?

Can a standard product be found which will be usable?

> "YOU NEVER KNOW, UNTIL YOU LOOK, JUST WHERE YOU WILL FIND NOT ONLY A SOLUTION TO ONE OF YOUR CURRENT PROBLEMS, BUT NEW IDEAS THAT WILL GIVE YOU FRESH APPROACHES TO MANY PROBLEMS.

FOR THE MAN WHO'S LOOKING FOR....

USE THE CREATIVE-PROBLEM-SOLVING TOOLS AND TECHNIQUES

IF YOU ARE DOING IT THE WAY YOU HAVE ALWAYS DONE IT —— IT PROBABLY IS WRONG.

THERE'S ALWAYS A BETTER WAY - FIND IT!

Twenty-Two Techniques for Problem-Solving

1. Creative Thinking
2. The Creative-Engineering Job Plan
3. Overcoming Roadblocks
4. Using Specialty Products, Processes, and Materials
5. Using Consistent Costs
6. Identifying the Function
7. Evaluating the Function
8. Evaluating by Comparison
9. Getting All the Facts—New and Old
10. Getting All Your Information from the Best Sources
11. Improving Human Relations
12. Blast Creating—Then Refining
13. Getting a Dollar Sign on the Key Tolerance
14. Putting a Dollar Sign on the Main Idea
15. Using Your Own Judgment
16. Spending the Company's Money as You Would Your Own
17. Using the Company's Services and Specialties
18. Working on Specifics—Not Generalities
19. Using Standards
20. Overcoming Habits and Attitudes
21. Using Positive Thinking
22. Using Teamwork

SUCCESS-FAILURE SYNDROME

All through life we are taught that failure is bad. All through school, children are constantly taught that it is bad to fail.

Finally, the child leaves school, and, if he becomes a scientist, for example, failure becomes a commonplace situation. The scientist knows that each failure is a step closer to success.

As Charles Kettering believed, when you desire to improve on something, let the invention invent itself. Ask what is necessary and through failures, success will appear.

It is an ironic situaton that this role reversal takes place in the lives of our children as they enter the work world.

Wouldn't it be better if we taught our children from the time they enter school that failure is the road to success? Wouldn't this be a better psychology to develop in our children than the success-failure syndrome of the present and the past?

Can you imagine a school where a child were praised because he failed to give the right answer and then were shown that then because he had failed, he was a step closer to success?

Wouldn't this process then help to develop better problem-solvers and better approaches to problem-solving than we now have in our education system?

V

Problem-Solving Techniques

In the process of solving problems, the creative mind is to be used. This is the mind that visualizes, foresees, analyzes, and creates.

In order to apply the creative mind to the problem-solving procedure, we have to learn the techniques available to train the mind. Such a method is creative manipulation. We can use the following methods to aid in problem-solving.

These methods use idea-spurring questions, adaptation, modification, substitution, addition, multiplication, subtraction, rearrangement, reversal, and combination.

SOME METHODS

The Edison Technique—Let the invention invent itself. To use this method one must continually ask questions of the item to be invented. You must ask what it needs to complete itself.

The Einstein Technique—Let the mind enter into the problem and it will find the solution. Einstein used to sit for hours looking almost dead. He was off in space analyzing the faults in his theory of relativity.

The Imagineering Technique—Suspend judgment temporarily, and let imagination soar; then engineer it back to earth.

The Bill Gordon Technique—Carefully select people to work on the project led by a chairman who is creative and knowledgeable about the subject.

The Dr. Paul Torrence Technique—Invent your own technique and use it. Accomplish what you want in the easiest possible manner.

TESTS OF CREATIVE ABILITY

I. *Concerning each of the following three items, indicate as many possible results of the situation and fill in with as many details as you wish.*

A. An airplane makes a forced landing in a jungle. There is plenty of food for the passengers, but the radio is out of order and the plane is unable to take off.

B. An elderly night watchman in a chemical plant discovers a fire when making his rounds. On his way to turn in an alarm he has a heart attack.

C. A workman repairing a house discovers a stamped but unmailed letter behind a baseboard. He drops it in the mail on the way home.

II. *Here are a number of statements which you will assume to be true. Give as many reasons or explanations as you can to explain the truth of these statements.*

A. More people have dental work done during February than any other month.

B. The proportion of bald-headed men living in New York State is greater than in Ohio.

C. In general, potatoes grown near rivers are smaller than those grown elsewhere.

D. There are proportionately more houses painted white in San Francisco than in Boston.

III. *Three common objects are named below. List all the pos-*

sible uses to which these objects might be put. (Give uses
that you have seen and uses that you can imagine.)

A. An empty beer can
B. A wooden clothespin
C. A sheet of 8½" × 11" paper
D. A red brick

IV. Answer whether you consider each of these statements
true or false.

A. I don't like to work on a problem unless there is the
possibility of coming out with a clear-cut and unam-
biguous answer.

B. I get sort of annoyed with writers who go out of their
way to use strange and unusual words.

C. For most questions, there is just one right answer, once
a person is able to get all the facts.

D. I would like to hear a great singer in an opera.

E. Compared to my own self-respect, the respect of others
means very little.

F. I would like to be a foreign correspondent for a news-
paper.

G. Every boy ought to get away from his family for a
year or two while he is still in his teens.

INCUBATION is a process by which the subconscious is allowed to
work on the problem.

SYNTHESIS is a process by which the parts of the problem are put
back together again in final form.

EVALUATION is the process of determining the value of the solution or solutions.

DEVELOPMENT includes the presentation and implementation of
evaluated solutions.

Note that in actual problem-solving we may combine some
of the above steps into one step. The process of observation,

definition, and preparation is sometimes called orientation. Further, we rarely follow the sequence in a one-two-three manner. While we are still defining the problem, our minds sometimes leap ahead making guesses at possible solutions. We do the same when we are still trying to analyze the problem.

Note that this classification of the steps in problem-processing is merely a *method of talking about the process* and is not actually *the thinking process itself*. However, such verbal behavior that is, generalizations as guides for action concerning specifics, can be helpful, and we will investigate these generalizations in detail.

SUPPLEMENT

Creative Manipulation

Listed below are categories in creative manipulation:

> Idea-spurring questions
> Adaptation
> Modification
> Substitution
> Addition
> Multiplication
> Subtraction
> Rearrangement
> Reversal
> Combination

In the exercises that follow, add ideas to the examples given.

Idea-Spurring Questions

Nothing unlocks secrets like questions. A favorite statement of Niels Henrick David Bohr, the famous Danish physicist, was, "Everything I utter should not be considered an affirmation but a question." If we want answers, we must ask questions.

1. List all the different questions you can ask about a brick:
   What is its size?
   What is it made of?

....

....

....

....

....

....

....

2. List all the different questions you can ask when evaluating
   subordinate:
   1. What kind of job does he do?
   2. Can he do the job better?

....

....

....

....

....

....

....

3. List questions you can ask about a chair:
   1. Why is it flat?
   2. Why does it have four legs?

....

....

....

....

....

....

Adaptation

Edison said that, "Your idea needs to be original only in its adaptation to the problem you are working on." Actually, it is the rare invention which is more than 5 percent new.

1. List all the questions you can that exploit adaptation:
   1. What does this suggest?
   2. Is there something similar to copy?

....

....

....

....

....

....

2. List ways that the characteristics of a paper pack of matches might be used:
   1. It may be bent and used for an ash tray
   2. It may be bent and used for a pencil holder

   ....

   ....

   ....

   ....

   ....

   ....

   ....

3. List ways the characteristics and/or functions of a lazy susan might be used:
   1. Serving hospital patients by test equipment
   2. Making items more available by permitting storage in a small space

   ....

   ....

   ....

   ....

   ....

   ....

   ....

4. List the characteristics and/or functions of a pair of pliers:
   1. As a hanger on a peg board
   2. As calipers

....

....

....

....

....

....

....

Modification

1. List questions which can be asked to modify something:
   1. How can this be altered?
   2. Can we twist it?

....

....

....

....

....

....

....

2. List ways to modify a car to improve riding quality:
   1. Three axles instead of two
   2. Air cushion seats

....

....

....

....

....

....

....

3. List ways to modify a telephone to improve it:
   1. Make it portable
   2. Include amplification

....

....

....

....

....

....

....

4. List ways to modify a swimming pool to improve it:
   1. Eliminate smooth walkways
   2. Use solar energy for heating

   ....

   ....

   ....

   ....

   ....

   ....

   ....

5. List ways to modify the internal communications of your company to increase efficiency:
   1. Instruct employees to listen
   2. Use written orders

   ....

   ....

   ....

   ....

   ....

   ....

   ....

Substitution

1. List questions which exploit substitution:
   1. What other processes will work?
   2. Where else?

....

....

....

....

....

....

....

2. List substitutions for auto chains:
   1. Ropes
   2. Metal slots

....

....

....

....

....

....

....

3. List substitutions for gasoline:
   1. Liquid air
   2. Methanol

   ....

   ....

   ....

   ....

   ....

   ....

   ....

4. List substitutions for strikes, i.e., ways to force management
   to negotiate:
   1. Slowdowns
   2. Arbitration

   ....

   ....

   ....

   ....

   ....

   ....

   ....

5. List substitutions for the phrase (usually used with children),
   "Don't do that!"
   1. "Stop doing that!"
   2. "Why are you doing that?"

....

....

....

....

....

....

....

Addition

1. List questions which can be asked to exploit addition:
   1. How can I combine the items?
   2. Are more of these necessary?

....

....

....

....

....

....

....

2. List features you could add to a car to make it more salable:
   1. Make it fly
   2. Add longer wearing tires

   ....

   ....

   ....

   ....

   ....

   ....

   ....

3. List what you might add to a football game to get more customers:
   1. Have giveaways at gate
   2. Honor players' families

   ....

   ....

   ....

   ....

   ....

   ....

   ....

4. List things you might add to ice cream to add more eye
   appeal:
   1. Fruit topping
   2. Nuts

   ....

   ....

   ....

   ....

   ....

   ....

   ....

5. List things you might add to a suit of clothes:
   1. More pockets
   2. Hidden pockets

   ....

   ....

   ....

   ....

   ....

   ....

   ....

Multiplication

1. List questions that exploit multiplication:
   1. Should we do it more often?
   2. Why not make them fatter?

   ....

   ....

   ....

   ....

   ....

   ....

2. List characteristics or functions of a school, which, if multiplied, would improve education.
   1. Bring lessons into home through TV
   2. Have TV monitors on the school bus

   ....

   ....

   ....

   ....

   ....

   ....

3. List things which might be improved by exaggeration:

    1. Behavior of a school class
    2. Production schedules

    ....

    ....

    ....

    ....

    ....

    ....

    ....

4. What might we multiply to improve the chances for peace? List them:

    1. Communication
    2. Understanding

    ....

    ....

    ....

    ....

    ....

    ....

    ....

5. What characteristics or functions of a TV can we maximize
   to improve? List them:
   1. Sound
   2. Clarity

....

....

....

....

....

....

Subtraction

1. List questions which exploit subtraction:
   1. What if this were smaller?
   2. How about dividing?

....

....

....

....

....

....

2. List things one might subtract from one's daily expenses to
   save money:
   1. Reduce heat during the day
   2. Turn lights off if not needed

   ....

   ....

   ....

   ....

   ....

   ....

   ....

3. List ways to minimize household chores:
   1. Organize the house
   2. Automate the vacuum

   ....

   ....

   ....

   ....

   ....

   ....

   ....

4. List things which should be miniatures:
   1. Dogs
   2. Cats

....

....

....

....

....

....

....

Rearrangement

1. List questions which exploit arrangement:
   1. What if the order were changed?
   2. How might the layout be better?

....

....

....

....

....

....

....

2. List things which might be better if rearranged:
   1. House furniture
   2. Production schedules

....

....

....

....

....

....

....

3. List things you might rearrange in your company to improve
   efficiency:
   1. The furniture
   2. The office layout

....

....

....

....

....

....

....

4. List ways you might rearrange your daily routine to enjoy
   life more:
   1. Taking time to think
   2. Exercising daily

....

....

....

....

....

....

....

Reversal

1. List questions which exploit reversal:
   1. Should it be vice versa?
   2. What are the opposites?

....

....

....

....

....

....

....

2. List things which might be improved by reversal:
   1. Work schedules
   2. Recreation schedules

....

....

....

....

....

....

3. What processes in your company might be better if reversed? List them:
   1. Pay scales
   2. Retirement schedules

....

....

....

....

....

....

....

4. List things in the government which might be better reversed.
   1. Taxes
   2. Manpower

....

....

....

....

....

....

....

Combination

1. Combination is perhaps the most exploited creative manipulation. List questions which exploit it:
   1. Can we combine?
   2. Can both parts fit together?

....

....

....

....

....

....

....

2. List things which might be combined with a cigarette lighter
   to make it more salable:
   1. Combine pack cigarettes with lighter?
   2. Combine lighter with cigarette case?

....

....

....

....

....

....

....

3. List household articles that could be combined:
   1. Combine sweeper with shampoo attachment
   2. Combine refrigerator with stove

....

....

....

....

....

....

....

4. List business or industrial practices or processes that might be profitably combined:
   1. Shipment of merchandise
   2. Purchasing practices

....

....

....

....

....

....

....

VI

Major Creative Techniques for Idea Development

The other day I was explaining to my children the difference between the directions of down and up, in an attempt to explain somewhat the principles behind Einstein's theory of relativity. If you will, draw a circle and depict this circle as the earth, showing, at either end, a picture to designate a man. Now, looking at this picture, how can we define what is down and what is up? To the man on one side of the earth, up is in the same direction as what the man on the other side considers down. So we can conclude that up and down are relative terms, and direction depends on where we are in relation to other positions. I hesitate to use the word *fixed* position, because, according to the theory of relativity, there are no fixed positions. If we take the example of the picture of the earth, we could also say the reason we cannot define our position except in relation to other things is that the earth at the same time is revolving on its own axis, and the earth is also moving in relation to the moon, stars, and other planets.

So, at best, we can only define our positions relative to objects that are within our range of measurement. This is a short and possibly confusing explanation of the relativity concept as proposed by Einstein. I digress into this area to show you that if we are to look for problems or worry about things, we don't have to look very far to see situations over which we have little or no control.

97

The principle to learn here is that you should concern yourself with those things about which you can do something and not worry about the things over which you have little or no control.

Another principle that we can learn here is that we should be leery of things which we see or hear until we have a chance to analyze them and learn what the truth is about the situation. What you are learning in this book are not only methods by which you can solve your personal problems but also methods by which you can determine what the facts or truths in a particular situations are and methods to determine what the value of certain decisions is, concerning things in which you have an interest. For, if you can assimilate the concepts being taught here, you will certainly know better how to define problems, search out the facts in a situation, come up with ideas, make decisions, and, most important, how to implement decisions that are made.

NURTURING POTENTIAL CREATIVITY

Creative talent can be developed—even an average potential can be developed by exercise. Many people have doubled their powers of recall. Like muscles and organs, intelligence and moral sense become atrophied for want of exercise. Creative power can be retained or regained, and it can be actually stimulated into growth. It is debatable whether what native creative talent one has can be added to, but it is certain that what one already has can be brought out into reality.

1. Experience provides fuel for ideation. The richest fuel for ideation is experience. Firsthand experience provides the very richest fuel; secondhand experience provides thinner fuel.

Travel tends to feed the imagination. The more you depend on yourself, the more you are able to think up ideas. Travel tends to open our minds. For the same reason, teachers of kindergartens and of lower grades are creative to an exceptional degree.

2. Playing games—solving puzzles induces creativity. There are more than three hundred sedentary games, only about fifty of which entail creative exercises. Checkers is a very creative game. Fishing involves creativity. Puzzle-solving is creative. Creating and decipering codes is creative.

3. Handicrafts improve creativity. Most other hobbies are collecting odd things; there is no creativity in that. The fine arts call for imagination. Painting and drawing put imagination through its paces.

4. Creativity thrives on reading—Francis Bacon said, "Reading maketh a full man." Our imaginations are whetted by the right kind of fiction. Short stories are short because they leave much to the imagination. The most rewarding form of reading is biography.

5. Writing is a creative exercise—Scientific tests rate facility in writing as a basic index of creative aptitude. We need not be born authors to write. Surveys tell us that 2.5 million Americans write for money. If we use our imagination, rejections need not cause dejection. Exercise imagination through word play.

6. Practice in Creative Problem-Solving—the most direct way to develop creativity is by practicing creativity. As a rule, instructor lecturing has been subordinated to student participation in the form of active problem-solving. Tests show those who took courses in problem-solving were able to average 94 percent better in production of ideas.

Overcoming Roadblocks—Mental Blocks

a. Perceptual—sometimes prevents us from seeing the obvious
b. Emotional—fear of failure, fear of making a mistake
c. Cultural—prevents us from departing from tradition

It is important to ask for what you desire. Let your imagination soar, then engineer it back to earth. Combine application of knowledge with the imagination to bring out ideas. Ignorance or a lack of knowledge reduces creativity.

1. Criticism is ruled out: Allowing yourself to be critical at the same time you are being creative is like trying to get hot and cold water from one faucet at the same time. Ideas aren't hot enough; criticism isn't cold enough. Results are tepid. (Criticism is reserved for a later "screening" session.)

2. The wilder the ideas, the better: Even "off-beat," impractical suggestions may "trigger" in other panel members practical suggestions which might not otherwise occur to them.

3. Quantity is wanted: The greater the number of ideas, the greater likelihood of winners.

4. Combination and improvement are sought: Improvements by others on an idea give better ideas. Combining ideas leads to more and better ideas.

Idea-Spurring Questions

PUT TO OTHER USES? New ways to use as is? Other uses if modified?

ADAPT? What else is like this? What other ideas does this suggest?

MODIFY? Change meaning, color, motion, sound, odor, taste, form, shape? Other changes?

MAGNIFY? What to add? Greater frequency? Stronger? Larger? Plus ingredient? Multiply?

MINIFY? What to subtract? Eliminate? Smaller? Lighter? Slower? Split up? Less frequent?

SUBSTITUTE? Who else instead? What else instead? Other place? Other time?

REARRANGE? Other layout? Other sequence? Change pace?

REVERSE? Opposites? Turn it backward? Turn it upside down? Turn it inside out?

COMBINE? How about a blend, an assortment? Combine purposes? Combine ideas?

SUPPLEMENT

Define the Basic Function

Use Verbs and Nouns

Verbs: Work Functions

Support	Limit
Transmit	Produce
Hold	Maintain
Enclose	Bypass
Collect	Isolate
Conduct	Connect
Insulate	Withstand
Protect	Resist
Prevent	Transmit
Amplify	Couple
Rectify	Provide
Change	Reduce
Interrupt	Indicate
Shield	
Modulate	
Control	
Attract	
Emit	
Repel	
Filter	
Impede	
Induce	

Verbs: Sell Functions

Increase
Improve
Create
Establish
Reduce

Nouns: Measurable

Weight	Phase
Torque	Power
Load	Components
Oxidation	Condition
Light	Warning
Heat	Operation
Flow	Sound
Radiation	
Current	
Voltage	

Nouns: Nonmeasurable

Part
Device
Component
Article
Table
Damage
Circuit
Repair

Nouns: Qualitative

Beauty
Appearance
Convenience
Style
Prestige
Effect
Deterioration

What Is the Function?
Is the Function Really Necessary?

SPECIFICATIONS

Are specifications unrealistic?
Does it do more than specifications require?
Do specifications contain unnecessary requirements?

DESIGN

Are requirements justified?
Does it exceed the functional requirements?
Are all features necessary?
Is there a better way to perform the function?
Are tolerances unreasonable or too costly to maintain?
Is there something else available that can do the job better and/
    or at lower cost?

MATERIAL

Can a less costly material be used?
Is there a better material for the job?

MANUFACTURING METHODS AND PROCESSES

Can parts or operations be combined, simplified, or eliminated?
Are any nonfunctional or appearance-only items required (surface
    finishes, machining operations, etc.)?
Can any parts be made by a less costly method (cast, forged,
    welded, formed, etc.)?
Will changes to finish requirements reduce cost?
Is proper tooling being used (considering quantity to be made)?

THEORETICAL MODEL FOR THE COMPLETE
"STRUCTURE OF INTELLECT"

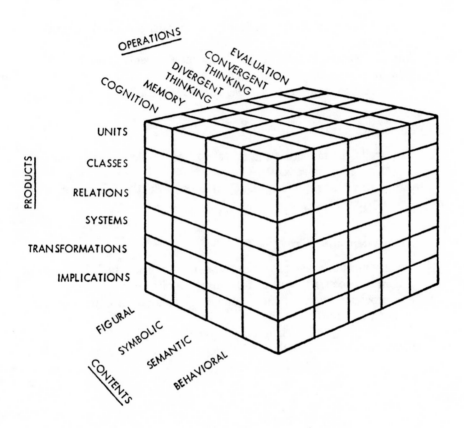

RELIABILITY, QUALITY, PERFORMANCE, MAINTAINABILITY

Can it be made simpler to improve reliability, quality, or maintainability?

Are quality and/or reliability higher than necessary to meet functional requirements?

Does it meet or exceed performance or environmental requirements?

Are all inspection, test, or qualifying requirements necessary?

Can maintainability be improved?

Can a change in material or design reduce weight?

PURCHASED ITEM

Can available standard parts or catalogued vendor parts be used or adapted at lower cost?

Can a specialty supplier product or process do the job better or at less cost?

DOCUMENTATION, OTHER

Do specification, test procedures and requirements include more than is necessary to meet functional requirements?

Are procedures clear, concise, and implemented with minimum time and effort?

Are packaging and/or handling requirements too high?

Can operation or installation be improved?

VII

Other Creative Techniques

MORPHOLOGICAL SYNTHESIS

Morphological synthesis is another device which aids in the production of ideas. This method of idea production relates more to the analysis than the synthesis of structure. Once a structure is analyzed to determine its component parts, then forced-relation techniques are used to produce ideas.

As an example of this procedure, let us use developing a promotion for a retail operation. In developing the promotion, we can consider three independent variables (1) the reason for the promotion; (2) the types of customers to be solicited; (3) the method of contact.

Under each heading you would think up a number of ideas, then relate each idea in each heading with each other heading. In this way a number of possible ideas or combinations could be produced.

The number of variables to be cross related could be increased, depending on the problem at hand. In this way we can use our imaginations to think up relationships between the variables associated with the solution to the problem, so that the ideas produced can be varied and many.

EDISON-KETTERING TECHNIQUES

The Edison technique called for trying anything and everything. Edison believed that the essence of scientific experimentation called for plenty of variation. Kettering was another who

105

believed that you should try one thing after another until the invention tells the inventor what it needs.

Kettering believed in endlessly piling up alternatives until success could be achieved.

As we have said in the previous chapters, when roadblocked on a project, it is necessary to review and counterreview. Analyze the problem statement again to see if the correct problem is being attacked. Break down the problem into simpler elements or restate it in a different way so that a new perspective is gained. In this way you will be, in effect, using the Edison-Kettering techniques to solve problems.

BIONICS

This is the study of how nature works. In solving problems associated with the world around us, it is wise to know the way nature works. In this way we can creatively attack our problems that relate to the world around us, for surely, if we ignore natural processes in problem-solving, we are ignoring available methods of solving problems.

As an example, if we are trying to develop a better strain of corn, we must know all about how natural processes affect the growth of corn. In this way, we are taking advantage of available knowledge against which we can test new ideas.

SYNECTIC ANALOGIES

The synectic approach to idea production as an aid to solving problems was developed by William Gordon. This approach divides a problem into two general phases. We first make the strange familiar by analyzing and studying all elements of the problem until we understand it as if it were commonplace. Then, to develop unique solutions, we make the strange familar by exploiting some "apparent irrelevancy" to evoke a new viewpoint. For example, we can think up uses for a pencil as other than a pencil by listing attributes that appear irrelevant. Then we pick one of the attributes and think up uses for that attribute.

ATTRIBUTE LISTING

This is a method developed by Prof. Robert P. Crawford. The person attacking the problem lists all of the various attributes of the idea or object. He then looks at each attribute and devises a checklist. To improve on the idea or problem, one must focus on each attribute and think up variations so as to improve the object or solve the problem, such as listing the attributes of a mousetrap, and then focusing on each part in order to improve the mousetrap.

CRAWFORD SLIP-WRITING

This is another aspect of the attribute-listing method of problem-solving. All of the attributes are listed on slips of paper, and the slips are looked at individually and submitted to creative questioning. In this way one can determine those things that are necessary to the object or idea and those that are superfluous. When the object or problem is reduced to its essence, the problem-solver can rebuild the object or problem in a creative manner so as to solve the problem or achieve a new and better object.

The Synectic Process

1. In general, the synectic approach developed by William J. Gordon, divides any problem into two general phases. It claims that first we:
   a. *Make the strange familiar;* that is, we analyze and study all elements of the problem until we understand its commonplace aspects.

   Then, in order to develop new unique solutions, we:

   b. *Make the familiar strange;* that is, we expoit some "apparent irrelevancy" to evoke a new viewpoint.

Morphological Analysis

A Creative Technique Worksheet
The Analysis and Synthesis of Structure

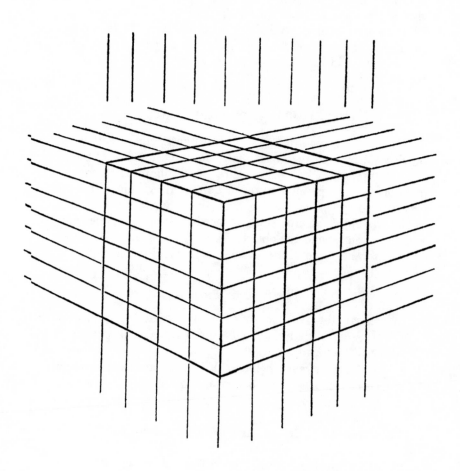

2. In thinking up uses for a pencil other than as a pencil, list the attributes of the pencil which appear to you as irrelevant.

eraser
metal clip holding eraser

3. Pick one of the irrelevant attributes listed above and list possible uses of that attribute.

eraser for bumper

Value Questions

1. What *function* does our *customer want or need?*
2. What function do we want to accomplish?
3. Is the function necessary?
4. What are the present and/or estimated costs of this function?
5. What *target cost* should *we set to make or buy* for overall system, subsystem, circuits, and components?
6. What *alternate ways* might we perform this function?
7. How much will each alternate cost?
8. What critique should we establish to test and verify alternates?
9. What are the measured variables of each specification requirement and is it necessary?
10. What is the function actually required to do?
11. What is the minimum tolerance safety factor?
12. How can we optimize the design in regard to producibility of product?
13. What else would improve, modify, combine, adapt, magnify, substitute, rearrange, reverse?
14. What is the best value-comparing *price, performance, reliability, time, delivery, salability,* and so forth?
15. In what ways might we implement the idea?
16. Who might do it?
17. When might it be done?
18. Where might it be done?
19. How might it be done?
20. Whom do I need to convince of its value?

Creative Exercise

Without lifting your pencil from the paper, draw four straight, connected lines which will go through all nine dots, but through each dot only once. After you have tried two different ways, ask yourself what restrictions you set up for yourself in solving this problem.

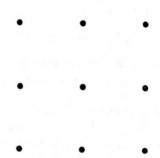

Nothing was mentioned about *not* extending the line beyond the dots.

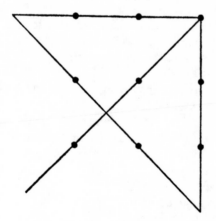

VIII

The Conscious and Subconscious Mind

Reality surrounds us, and we are surrounded and bombarded with impressions on a continuous basis. During our working hours, we rely on our conscious mind to give us the data we need to get us through the day. But all of the time our subconscious is also working. A distinguished mathematician, John Von Neuman, believed in what he called the subconscious. He said that he often went to bed at night with an unsolved problem on his mind and upon waking was able to put the answer on his scratch pad beside the bed.

In literature, the same thing has happened to countless authors of the past. Modern authors have similarly attested that a story must simmer in its own juice for months or even years before it is ready to serve.

Modern science recognizes the productivity of illumination. Dr. Walter B. Cannon of Harvard, after forty years in research, wrote, "From the years of my youth, the unearned assistance of sudden and unpredicted insight has been common." His investigation of the creative habits of over two hundred chemists revealed that over a third of these scientists gave credit to hunches. Many scientists of the past likewise stressed illumination. These have included Darwin, Hamilton, Poincare and others.

We call the creative process that calls for little or no conscious effort *incubation* (or purposive relaxation). Incubation applied to the workings of imagination covers the process by which ideas "spontaneously" well up into our consciousness.

Incubation many times results in bright ideas and has been known as "the period of luminous surprise." John Masefield, Henry James, Emerson, Shakespeare, and Somerset Maugham all have commented on incubation as it relates to their success. All have considered it important.

Analysis of creative thinking by all who have studied the process has led to the conclusion that four stages are evident. These are: preparation, or the gathering of relevant information and attempting to organize it; incubation, a period of relative inactivity, perhaps with recurrence of ideas about the problem, but no evident progress; inspiration, the sudden illumination or "that's-the-answer" experience; and verification, or revision, the testing out and evaluation of the idea inference, or hypothesis, either by implicit processes or by actual experiment. While this explanation gives importance to the subconscious, it negates idea-finding. Without ideas, problems would be difficult to solve.

Creative thinking thrives on enthusiasm, and this tends to lag when we force ourselves; therefore you will find that, by letting up for a while, we tend to regenerate our capacity to correlate ideas, solve problems, and come up with new ideas. A positive approach is always necessary in approaching problems. Believe that all things are possible. It has been said that illumination, like life, will always remain a mystery.

In our brain we have over three billion cells each with a capacity to hold information or channel it into different directions. These cells are more than all of the electrical circuits in North America. Therefore, you can appreciate that the brain of man is more complex than any computer produced so far—probably than any computer that ever will be produced.

Sleep, above all else, helps court illumination, for it tends to step up our power of association as well as to recharge our mental energy.

Creative people have their own methods of illumination at times such as while getting a haircut, taking a nap, stargazing, sleeping, deliberately sustaining silence, sitting still, shifting activity, switching projects or working on several simultaneously, taking a walk, buying a new hat, playing the piano, going to church. These and countless other methods are used by creative people in prodding the subconscious into doing its work.

It is a general opinion that ideas, once they appear, should be noted. An idea is a fleeting thing and once lost may never be regained. All ideas in trying to solve a problem should be recorded. It has been said that the stream of ideas flows continuously during all of our waking hours, and along this stream priceless ideas are passing. The thing to do is to gather them as they go by; jotting down ideas and looking them over stimulates the production of other ideas.

It is true that nothing is new under the sun. Most ideas are combinations or improvements upon other ideas. A creative thinker evolves new combinations of ideas already in his mind.

IX

Workshop Techniques—
a Comparative Study
of the Welfare
and Social Security
Systems

We will discuss an actual case solved by the creative-problem-solving procedure that was done in the classroom. This study involves a correlation of the welfare system with the Social Security system.

BACKGROUND INFORMATION

Arrangements were made with a Mr. Smith from the Social Security office to explain the role and workings of Social Security. Mr. Smith distributed the following pamphlets after his discussion on Social Security:

1. "Social Security Cash Benefits for Students 18-22"
2. "Disabled? Find Out If You Are Eligible for Social Security Disability Insurance Benefits"
3. "Your Social Security"
4. "Public Assistance in Pennsylvania"
5. "What You Should Know about Applying for Public Assistance in Pennsylvania"
6. "Food Stamp Program"

As additional background information for the project, the participants discussed current operations of the welfare system and

114

various proposed changes. Since the participants were from the community service agencies, they were able to relate to the current standards in Pennsylvania.

It was pointed out that there was no uniformity state to state regarding welfare benefits. In addition, the benefits varied so that subsistence on welfare in many states meant that the family had to exist below the national poverty level.

As further background information, various other matters were discussed including a proposal to revamp the welfare system. It was noted that at the time of this study in 1973 no efforts were under way in the United States to correlate the welfare program with Social Security.

In 1978, though a welfare program change has been proposed by the Carter Administration, no one has come forth with a plan to correlate Social Security with welfare benefits such as was the subject of the case study below.

Perhaps this study could give the administration in Washington something to think about in terms of savings.

In analyzing the background information, we came to this statement of the problem:

How can we correlate the Social-Security system more effectively with the Welfare system in the United States so as to more critically evaluate a person's right to welfare and whether or not a person is getting the maximum benefits to which he is entitled?

PROBLEM DEFINITIONS:
   That which assists financially = Welfare
   That which aids in retirement = Social Security

Questions regarding the Problem Statement:
1. What are the requirements for welfare and Social Security?
2. What is the people's conception regarding welfare and Social-Security benefits?
3. What correlation now exists between Social Security and welfare?
4. How are people evaluated for welfare rights?
5. What do we mean by *welfare?*

IDEATION

The following are ideas suggested as a possible solution for this problem:

1. Find a common definition of "disability."
2. Refer all welfare clients to Social Security before a determination is made.
3. Follow up to inform people of new programs.
4. Improve the attitudes of the Social-Security workers and the welfare caseworkers in regard to claimants.
5. Advertise the benefits available.
6. Include pamphlets in monthly check mailings.
7. Set up monthly meetings to discuss benefits.
8. Arrange panel shows to demonstrate how to overcome their difficulties.
9. Set up a pamphlet showing procedures for applying for Social-Security and welfare benefits.
10. Advertise through films at theaters.
11. Compile a directory of social services and benefits.
12. Educate the public.
13. Set up a federal system to insure equal benefits to all, regardless of place of residency.
14. Establish day-care centers.
15. Set up benefits similar to Social Security for welfare provisions.
16. Have an "intercommunication" program for Social Security and welfare people.
17. Set up definite criteria for Social Security and welfare applicants.
18. Increase the staff of Social Security.
19. Increase the competency of Social Security staff.
20. Increase the competency of welfare caseworkers.
21. Set up a federally administered program for welfare through the Social Security system.
22. Tie unemployment, Social Security, and welfare into one Federal system so that unemployed people automatically entitle themselves to benefits.
23. Standardize the welfare payments throughout the country.

When each idea was evaluated with the possibility of fifty (50) points, the results were as follows:

Criteria	(1) How it will Affect the Country	(2) How it Affects the Social Security Program	(3) How it Affects the Welfare Program	(4) Eligibility of the People	(5) Needs of the People	(6) Considering Both Sides of the Story	(7) How it will Affect the Budget	(8) How it will Affect the Recipients	(9) Timing of the Idea	(10) Funding of the Program	(11) Resources	(12) Availability	Total
1.	5	8	8	10	10	2	0	1	10	0	0	0	42
2.	0	10	10	10	10	0	0	0	7	0	0	0	37
3.	3	5	5	5	3	3	0	0	8	0	0	3	42
4.	10	10	10	10	3	2	2	2	0	0	0	0	38
5.	12	10	10	10	0	0	0	8	0	0	0	0	30
6.	5	5	5	5	0	0	5	0	8	0	0	0	35
7.	5	5	5	5	5	0	0	0	0	0	0	0	27
8.	5	5	1	5	0	0	10	0	0	0	0	0	45
9.	3	1	10	0	0	0	0	10	0	0	10	0	13
10.	10	5	1	10	0	0	2	5	0	0	0	5	50
11.	10	3	10	10	5	0	0	5	0	0	0	1	50
12.	15	10	10	0	2	0	0	10	0	0	0	5	50
13.	0	10	10	0	10	0	0	5	0	0	0	0	18
14.	10	10	0	0	0	0	0	12	0	0	0	0	50
15.	10	0	5	0	5	0	0	7	0	0	0	5	44
16.	5	0	10	0	5	0	0	10	0	0	5	3	37
17.	10	10	15	0	5	0	0	7	0	0	0	2	44
18.	10	0	0	5	5	5	0	7	0	0	0	7	44
19.	10	10	0	0	5	0	0	0	0	0	0	7	47
20.	10	10	0	10	5	5	0	10	7	0	0	10	47
21.	15	0	12	0	5	0	0	0	0	0	0	5	47
22.	10	10	10	10	10	10	0	0	0	0	0	0	50
23.	10	0	10	0	10	0	0	15	0	0	0	5	50

The ideas with the highest scores and the greatest possibilities of success were 5—11—12—13—15—22—23

EVALUATION OF IDEAS

The ideas suggested were evaluated according to the following criteria:

1. How it will affect the country
2. How it affects the Social Security program
3. How it affects the welfare program
4. Eligibility of the people
5. Needs of the people
6. Considering both sides of the story
7. How it will affect the budget
8. How it will affect the recipients
9. Timing of the idea
10. Funding of the program
11. Resources
12. Availability

PLAN OF IMPLEMENTATION

1. Prepare an up-to-date directory listing all social services.
2. Include pamphlets in daily paper and Sunday supplements.
3. Give pamphlets to all applicants for social security or welfare.
4. Place posters around area.
5. Put on television and radio.
6. Place copies in hospitals and other public places.
7. Mail pamphlets to all applicants.
8. Have speakers go to meetings and speak on subject.
9. Have Congress enact law to set up benefits for welfare that are similar to social security.
10. Have Congress enact law to tie systems together.
11. Enact a broad, standard, federal-welfare law through Congress. Include under this food stamps, free school-lunch program, and other aid program, such as medical.
12. Notify congressmen of possibilities.
13. Notify Social Security program of possibilities.
14. Notify welfare department of possibilities.

X

The Evaluation Phase

Previously, it was mentioned that the evaluation phase is sometimes called the judgment phase. In this step of the problem-solving process, we are examining all of the ideas to determine which is the best to solve our problem as defined in the first step of the problem-solving process.

EVALUATIVE CRITERIA

The evaluative criteria are the yardsticks by which the ideas are measured. These evaluative criteria are used to test and verify the strength of your ideas. The criteria are really a further measure of the problem-solver's sensitivity to the problem.

The evaluative criteria are used to anticipate all the effects and consequences that can occur in accomplishing a solution to the problem as defined.

In trying to establish evaluative criteria you should ask questions about the ideas, such as, "What might be affected?" or "Who might be affected?"

All the ideas should be tested for consistency with the facts.

It is important to choose carefully and select evaluative criteria that will thoroughly test the ideas against reality. The better the evaluative criteria, the better ideas or decisions will evolve from the evaluation phase.

Questions such as the following could be used as evaluative criteria:

119

1. Effect on quality
2. Effect on cost
3. Effect on equipment
4. Time to implement
5. Testing required

These are only samples of potential evaluative criteria. It is important to choose the evaluative criteria carefully to insure the best decisions.

Refining Your Ideas

Another way to narrow down your ideas for final evaluation and decision-making is a procedure by which the ideas are listed and the advantages and disadvantages listed with a rating schedule. The rating schedule would have such criteria as immediate use, rejection, modification, or "hold for later evaluation."

This procedure of refining your ideas will allow you to narrow down your final evaluation chart. This then will allow you to pick the best ideas as your decisions for immediate action.

The refining of your ideas is just as important in the problem-solving process as any other step.

Evaluation Phase Form

In order to have a consistency of operation in problem-solving, it is important to set a standard form for the evaluation of your ideas. A suggested form is shown in one of the examples of a problem-solving report shown in workshop techniques. This format lists the ideas in vertical fashion at the left of the page with the evaluative criteria shown to the right in horizontal fashion. This creates blocks in which to rate each idea against each criterion. This allows you to total each idea quantity to the extreme right. Naturally the highest totals are our best ideas and become our best decisions.

XI

The Decision-Making Phase

Our ideas are our decisions when they are properly evaluated. It is in the evaluation phase that we must apply the critiques in an unbiased manner so as to arrive at the best decisions. If you will remember, we asked the question earlier, "Is there only one answer to a problem after all the facts are known?" We now realize, after reading this book, that there are many answers once the facts are known, and, as a captain of a ship must, you have to set the course to make the best decision possible. In order to do this, you must know as many of the facts as possible concerning the problem, or otherwise you would make the decision from ignorance. If you have many facts and then make a bad decision, you are making the bad decision through stupidity, because you have not applied the intelligence you possess to analyze the ideas completely before presenting a decision.

To be as correct as possible you must think, think, and think again. Lay the problem and the idea aside, and let them grow in the computer of your mind. You will find that your mind will diligently pursue the answer to your problem. Do not be afraid to ask for help, but ask from reliable or intelligent sources. A man, for instance, who knows nothing about chemistry is of little help in solving a chemical problem.

Search out the facts and bring them to bear on the problem. Ideas will almost spontaneously emerge from your mind on how to solve the problem.

Apply the techniques you have learned in this book, and you will find that there is no problem to which a solution cannot be found. The basic reason people become confused and morose when a problem occurs is that they lack knowledge concerning procedures of how to attack and solve the problem.

It is as true today as it was from the beginning of man's existence on earth that each working day creates problems, and, the more complex society becomes, the more problems come to the forefront.

Face each problem confidently and positively, and you will persevere to find the solution that will ease your mind.

XII

The Implementation Phase

The final phase of problem-solving is the implementation phase.

After all the work of defining the problem, coming up with ideas, evaluating the ideas, and making the decisions is complete, the final step, which is most important, is to implement your decisions.

One of the steps in implementing your decision is the report which tells what you have done.

In order to prepare a proper report, a procedure must be followed. Suggestions for a report are as follows:

1. Select a title. Then refer to the item, process, or assembly under study; summarize the problem; and give proposed solution.
2. Clarify what the item or process is, what it does, and where it fits into the whole picture.
3. Indicate why it was selected for study.
4. Show why savings are likely.
5. Reveal ultimate use, and provide short description of salient features. Indicate in detail the savings would result.
6. Summarize the pattern of study.
7. Where appropriate, name the contributors in the organization—you can't give away credit. If it has approval of other people, cite them.
8. Design report to secure approval.

9. Samples, charts, figures, and tables are good, as are illustrations and photos. You should have a table of contents in a long report.
10. Tailor explanations to the experience level of the reader.
11. At higher administrative levels, the savings picture will be much more meaningful.

HOW TO SELL IDEAS

Once a proposal is submitted, it must be followed up to be put in to action. Prime responsibility for a creative proposal is up to you. Delay in project acceptance means a loss in savings or possible abandonment of the project. Your final proposal must be short and concise. A summary statement is usually much more desirable. Overselling is just as bad as underselling, so you must clearly state what you are selling and the advantages of your proposal.

To be a success, you must communicate with other people: "I want to get people to do what I want done but because they want to do it."

Everyone of us sometimes has to be a salesman to get things done. Getting people to accept an idea is selling. All through life we are trying to get people to do things because they want to do it.

Questions to Ask Yourself

1. What am I trying to accomplish?
2. What do I want someone to do?
3. What can it do for him personally? (Know your prospect.) Highlight portion of presentation that is acceptable. Talk about what acceptor is interested in.
4. What benefits can I make obvious to him? Input is features; output is benefits.
5. What roadblocks do I have to overcome?
6. Who, what, where, how? (That will start accomplishments to start positive action.)

7. What can I do to make sure of following up to guarantee successful closing of accomplishment?

The KISS Factor—"Keep It Simple, Salable."

Briefness is important in reports. Remember that simplicity means making it "short and sweet."

Another Method Is to Construct a Duties-and-Responsibilities Sheet

1. Has the customer specification been examined to determine if he is asking for more than he needs?
2. Has the cost for overdesign been assumed in the sales price?
3. Does the design give customer what he wants and no more?
4. Are the quantities built on the order known?
5. Does the circuit represent the optimum?

Find the simple solution first and then build on it. Define the function. Design for maximum simplicity of all functional and physical characteristics. Design for producibility to obtain optimum value of manufacturing methods or processes and question their inherent design limitations. Design for necessary quantity objective in tooling, manufacture, and so forth. Design for least possible number of manufacturing operations and quality-control situations.

PREPARING FOR REPORTS

1. The technical position of your company
2. New enthusiasm, innovation, inventiveness, vitality
3. Key personnel development
4. Future available capacity
5. Additional critiques

Closing is important—follow through each item to closing to the best of your ability. Developing ideas is good, but, if we leave it there, we frustrate ourselves. One must follow through and *implement* the decision. Persistence and patience are important in problem-solving. Sell softly but persistently in order to get acceptance.

GETTING THE SOLUTION ADOPTED

Selected Idea:

In what ways can I convince my boss that I should have a raise?
Whom do I need to convince of its value? (Maybe yourself!)
Senior Engineer
What do I want him to do about the idea?
*I want him to give me an 8 percent raise. I want him to accept
and follow through.* For example: authorize its use; buy the piece
of equipment; give me time off to develop it for production, and
so forth.

Give him the advantages of accepting the idea: If idea "tested"
well, these are some of the advantages:

1. One big advantage would be better cooperation from me, more
   satisfied employee.
2. Better attitude from me, more enthusiasm generated.
3. More industriousness from me, chance to criticize constructively.
4. I would be closer in salary to him and therefore would make a
   raise for him essential.

   Possible objections he may have to the idea:
1. The budget won't allow it. This is the wrong time to approach him.
2. I don't need the money. I am getting too much already.
   Haven't done good enough job.
3. I haven't been as cooperative as possible. Need a better attitude. Need to train technician better. Need to be less direct.

   How to make this advantage obvious to him:
(How to visualize it for him, how to present arguments con-
vincingly, and so forth.)

1. a. Show him how you would do a better job
   b. Tell him how well he does his job
   c. Show him an improved attitude
2. a. Show him improved enthusiasm
   b. Come up with at least one good idea
   c. Be more industrious
3. a. Be more cooperative
   b. Be happier in your job
   c. Think more constructively etc.
4. a. Show him you are company-minded
   b. Show him you are also interested in *his* progress

How to overcome his objections:
1. a. Show him that better men need to be better paid
   b. You need the money
2. a. You are not really ahead of other people
   b. You are trying to improve your work
   c. You are trying to be more cooperative
3. a. You are trying to develop better attitude
   b. You are trying to develop more ideas
   c. You are trying to be less direct

XIII

The Reporting Phase

In order to motivate positive action it is necessary to have an effective proposal. All of the previous work, including the identification of the problem, ideation, evaluation, and decision-making is for naught, unless an effective proposal for implementation is presented.

Certain guidelines should be followed in the writing of a creative-problem-solving-report. Specifically you should:

1. Think about the real effect of your words. You are trying to convince the people to whom you are presenting the report of its value; therefore, choose your words carefully. Analyze what effect each word might have on the reader.

2. Put yourself in the place of the reader. Empathy is important here. You must detach yourself in order to weigh the full effect of what you are reporting.

3. Use a clear, concise, journalistic approach. Report the facts and substantiate them as clearly as possible.

4. Try to emphasize precision and discipline. It is important that all of the data you present to justify your decision is accurate and not subject to misinterpretation.

5. Use an outline to build your report. In this way you will have a logical, coordinated package to present to your reader.

6. Examine methods that can improve your fluency.

7. Be sure the words or sentences you use tend to improve communication rather than cloud the issue.

8. Do not try to impress your reader with old, worn-out expressions. Stick to the facts.

Motivating Positive Action on Your Proposal

In order to effectively get your reader to consider adoption of your report, it is necessary to consider certain items in the preparation of an effective proposal:

1. The title must refer to the subject under study in a clear, concise manner. This should be followed by a summary of what the problem is and the proposed description of the solution.

2. Describe clearly the nature of the item or process and what it does. Try to fit it into the overall picture and give any facts that will describe more fully the subject of the proposal.

3. Discuss the reason for study of the problem and how you arrived at the problem. Show why the solution to the problem will benefit your organization and what savings might be involved.

4. Describe the alternative to adoption of your solution and what bad features might result from the alternative or inaction on your proposal.

5. If the solution to your problem will result in savings, then detail the savings that will result. If the solution will bring about some other beneficial effects, such as the elimination of a social problem or environmental problem, indicate the beneficial results.

6. Show how you began the study that led to your proposal and refer to the sources of your data.

7. If it is appropriate, mention other people who might have aided you in obtaining data. You can't give credit away, for it comes right back to you. If you can show that other people have approved of your action, cite the supporting factors.

8. Keep in mind that you desire the proposal to be approved. Anticipate any objections and provide the answers. Don't put yourself in the position of having inadequate documentation, for the reader does not want to have to seek other sources of information to bolster your case.

9. If your proposal is long and complex, try to use simple charts, figures, or tables to present the data, rather than pages of hard-to-read values, dates, and statistics. Photo and illustrations

are very helpful, and a table of contents is a necessity for a long proposal. The conclusion must be supported within the proposal.

10. Explanations are to be aimed at the training and experience level of the reader. While engineers might require technical details to approve your proposal, higher administration levels require emphasis on financial benefits. Long-range effect on policy and applications are more significant at higher levels of decision-making.

The Case for Brevity

The house Census and Government Statistics Subcommittee has been hearing testimony in its study of ways to reduce the paperwork burden of industry.

In an address to his fellow employees, the president of a corporation reminded them that the length of a communication is no guide to its importance. He illustrated this by the following examples:

> The Lord's Prayer—56 words
> Lincoln's Gettysburg Address—266 words
> Ten Commandments—297 words
> The 23rd Psalm—118 words
> U.S. Government on cabbage prices—26,911 words

There is no objection by business to necessary useful data, but we hear from many companies regarding thousands of reports of which many are mere duplications.

How to Effectively Deliver Your Presentation

Some of the proven techniques for presenting your proposal are:

1. Pause before opening your mouth—think before you speak.
2. Recognize your listeners—be aware of who is listening to your proposal.

3. Gain attention by various techniques, and then lead into your subject.
4. Try to put "fire" into some of your words and phrases to make a point.
5. When speaking, vary the tone or volume of your voice for emphasis.
6. Talk to the rear of the room; don't just concentrate on those up front.
7. Arrange a transition when someone else is to present a portion of the presentation.
8. Be sure to introduce any associate and the topics he might cover.
9. Wrap up the program in a definite manner when specialized portions are presented.
10. Get the audience active by asking for questions or asking them questions.
11. Try to transmit your enthusiasm for the concepts you are presenting to the audience.

Just as there are things you must do to present your proposal properly, so also is it important to avoid various things in your presentation. Some of the items to keep in mind are:

1. Avoid mumbling—Clarity of speech is important to the concept you are trying to get across to the audience.
2. Don't slur words or mispronounce them. This can cause misinterpretation or loss of a point in your presentation.
3. Avoid poor grammar and trite expressions.
4. Avoid the rise of "Ahs."
5. Don't resort to flattery or apology.
6. Don't keep your hands in the same position throughout your talk.
7. Don't fidget with your clothes or a pointer.
8. Don't read your presentation.
9. Don't be too long in presenting your proposal.
10. Don't read words on a chart that can be read by the audience.

11. Don't overcrowd your visual presentations with detailed data.
12. Don't pass out brochures during the presentation.
13. Don't have projection equipment without spare bulbs, fuses, and so forth handy.
14. Don't let your confidence or lack of it turn you into a ham.

We have examined some of the important things necessary for delivery of a proposal. As has been stated before, the proposal can be the start of a great project, or it can be the source of more material for the wastebasket. Following the guidelines presented can assure of greater success with your proposals.

Creative Fidelity and Its Relationship to Creative Problem-Solving

Recently a service club to which I belong had a speaker on fidelity. Faithfulness to someone or something also requires creativity. As we mentioned in problem-solving, to gain the final solution, one essential ingredient is a stick-to-it type of quality in the problem-solver. Roadblocks should be of no consequence to the problem-solver, for these are only alternative creators to him in his searching for a solution to the problem that is the task at hand.

All of our relationships with our fellow human beings require a certain amount of faith, and this faith is a transfer between inner selves, not outside material forces. It is the external force that tends to test this faithfulness to one another and test our stick-to-itiveness in solving problems.

SUMMARY AND OVERVIEW OF CREATIVE PROBLEM-SOLVING

They say there are three types of people in this world. The first type consists of the poor unfortunate: the mentally ill, mentally retarded, those unexposed to civilization, and those who are by their own choice living in a world by themselves. All these constitute the first type of person who does not know what is happening in his surroundings.

The second type of person is the one who knows what is happening. He is the average person who does his daily work diligently. But, because of his many other problems, he cannot find time to notice very many things happening around him. For example, he notices a new church going up, a new office building, a new motel, a new street, new products in the paper, new historical events, but he is not concerned whether these things happen or not, nor does he generally influence the happenings.

Now, the third type of person is the creative person. He is the person who makes things happen. He is the one who comes up with the idea for the new product, the new building, the new motel, the new office building. He is a creative thinker and a doer.

You have the choice in life to be the type of person you want to be, and it is your decision as to what direction in life you want to take.

It is never too late to change your course, and, as someone else has said before, "You can be anything you want to be if you are willing to pay the price in sacrifice."

To answer our own question posed earlier, there is nothing that is impossible. The creative mind of man has no limits. It has infinite potential; the bounds of man's mind are limitless.

Decide now as a result of this book that you will never again take a negative attitude toward ideas.

Be cooperative and try to be positive at all times in regard to ideas or plans presented to you for your consideration. Remember that, if you are to be a leader, a thinker, or a problem-solver, you must encourage and find ways for other people to overcome their difficulties.

In summary, let us review briefly what we have learned in this book.

Our approach has been directed to a personal-problem-solving approach. Basically, most of our problems are of a personal nature, and it is in the approach we take to our problems that we give to others a picture of ourselves.

Creativity, the ability to come up with ideas, and the ability to solve problems are recognized by those who judge us.

In our approach to problems we show to others our maturity, intelligence, cooperativeness, perseverance, humility, and many other traits we possess. Whether we like it or not, we are constantly being appraised in regard to our abilities. Others see us as we are, while, vain creatures that we are, we see ourselves on a much more praiseworthy or higher level than we are seen.

Development of your own creative-problem-solving facility can only aid you in reaching your own potential, but we are speaking figuratively only, because we know from previous experience that no one can reach his ultimate potential. We can only strive toward what is sometimes called perfection, realizing that the ultimate is beyond our reach.

As I have said previously, the mind of man has a potentially unlimited capacity to do whatever it desires. It is man's body which limits his capacity, the material in which the mind of man is stored. It limits his progress and his deeds. But, without the material in which the mind is stored, you can realize man's potential more clearly. For, without the body, the mind can travel wherever it desires, through the far reaches of space, over boundless mountains and endless seas. The mystery is the entombment of the elusive mind in the material body. Whether it is in fact immaterial might be a debatable question, but its existence can be questioned only by an irrational being, for, if we can even discuss it, it then must exist in some form. Otherwise, we would not be capable of even discussing the situation; it would be academic.

PERSONAL IMPROVEMENTS DEVELOPED IN STUDYING CREATIVE PROBLEM-SOLVING

How to take a more objective view of my problems
How to use the best of all techniques to solve problems
How to improve confidence in my own judgment
How to apply imagination more effectively
How to eliminate roadblocks to success
How to use a creative systematic approach to problem-solving
How to make a most effective cost analysis of operations

How to make a more effective search and retrieval of data from the best sources

How to simplify and improve effectiveness of reports

How to realize that I have creative ability

How to get people to do what I want done because *they* want to do it

How to improve ability to communicate

How to organize facts

How to improve my enthusiasm

How to improve attitude and develop more confidence in my ability to come up with new ideas

How to develop a rational, systematic approach for attacking problems

How to improve confidence in the future of the company

How to be personally effective on my job

How to organize facts

How to improve openmindedness

How to listen creatively

How to observe for retention

How to synthesize more effectively

How to develop insight and intuitive ability

How to improve ability to innovate new products

How to invent for new patents

How to make an objective appraisal of my job

How to improve in leadership ability

How to improve my own self-confidence

How to evaluate by comparison

How to make more effective decisions

How to use the systems concept (overall look) to enlarge viewpoint

How to develop alternative ideas

How to develop patience with persistence in overcoming obstacles

How to build a target value model on every function

How to anticipate problems before they become hopeless

How to ask a creative question for an objective attack on problems

How to broaden thinking

How to develop awareness that problems are creative golden opportunities

How to simplify function and apply the KISS factor

How to improve in all management skills

How to weigh and decide by making nine comparative evaluation matrices of critique *vs.* ideas

How to develop a critique to verify and test ideas

How to recognize when I am a roadblock to someone else's ideas

How to improve engineering and management skills

How to put teams in management

How to avoid assuming facts

How to be sensitive to customer product value

How to be sensitive to problems

How to get information from the best sources

How to be fluent with ideas

How to improve initiative and drive

How to put a dollar sign on all functions

How to be flexible in attitude

How to improve attitude

How to improve ability to sell ideas

How to select and make decisions on ideas

How to present ideas to management

How to develop reasoning ability

How to abstract facts from opinions

How to develop cost sensitivity

How to redefine skill

How to develop persistence to close ideas

How to overcome roadblocks

How to ask the right questions for the right answers

How to improve knowledge of creative-idea-stimulation techniques

How to define and simplify function

How to define and clarify problems

How to secure help on problems

How to defer judgment when creating ideas

Printed in the United States
71214LV00006B/203

9 781583 487235